THE
ESSENTIAL
CASTLE

Other Works by Valerie Estelle Frankel

Henry Potty and the Pet Rock: A Harry Potter Parody

Henry Potty and the Deathly Paper Shortage: A Harry Potter Parody

Buffy and the Heroine's Journey

From Girl to Goddess: The Heroine's Journey in Myth and Legend

Katniss the Cattail: The Unauthorized Guide to Name and Symbols

The Many Faces of Katniss Everdeen: The Heroine of The Hunger Games

Harry Potter, Still Recruiting: A Look at Harry Potter Fandom

Teaching with Harry Potter

An Unexpected Parody: The Spoof of The Hobbit Movie

Teaching with Harry Potter

Myths and Motifs in The Mortal Instruments

Winning the Game of Thrones: The Host of Characters & their Agendas

Winter is Coming: Symbols, Portents, and Hidden Meanings in A Game of Thrones

Bloodsuckers on the Bayou: The Myths, Symbols, and Tales Behind HBO's True Blood

The Girl's Guide to the Heroine's Journey

Choosing to be Insurgent or Allegiant: Symbols, Themes & Analysis of the Divergent Trilogy

Doctor Who and the Hero's Journey: The Doctor and Companions as Chosen Ones

Doctor Who: The What Where and How

Sherlock: Every Canon Reference You May Have Missed in BBC's Series

Symbols in Game of Thrones

How Game of Thrones Will End

Joss Whedon's Names

Pop Culture in the Whedonverse

Women in Game of Thrones: Power, Conformity, and Resistance

History, Homages and the Highlands: An Outlander Guide

The Catch-Up Guide to Doctor Who

Remember All Their Faces: A Deeper Look at Character, Gender and the Prison World of Orange Is The New Black

Everything I Learned in Life I Know from Joss Whedon

Empowered: Symbolism, Feminism, and Superheroism of Wonder Woman

The Avengers Face their Dark Sides

The Comics of Joss Whedon: Critical Essays

Mythology in Game of Thrones

Castle Loves Fandom: Celebrating the Detective Show's Quips, Homages, and Meta-Salutes

THE ESSENTIAL CASTLE

PLOTS, CHARACTERS, EPISODES AND NOVELS FROM THE ABC DETECTIVE SHOW

VALERIE ESTELLE FRANKEL

This book is an unauthorized guide and commentary on the *Castle* show and its associated comics and books. None of the individuals or companies associated with the comics, television show or any merchandise based on this series has in any way sponsored, approved, endorsed, or authorized this book.

ISBN-13: 978-0692548370 (LitCrit Press)
ISBN-10: 0692548378

Contents

THE ESSENTIAL CASTLE

Essential Castle

3XK, Jackson Hunt, Senator Bracken. All these names conjure explosive stories, stretching across multiple seasons. Here they're all laid out: character arcs, backstory, plot arcs – with all the details from beginning to end.

The novels and comics too get a look – those existing on real shelves and those only on Castle's website and in the minds of the writers. Learn about Detective Nikki Heat, Pulitzer prize winning journalist Jameson Rook, CIA agent Derrick Storm, bad girl Clara Strike, and everyone else in Castle's imaginary worlds. Trace the Castle-Beckett romance from the beginning and lovingly look over each wacky Castle theory. With nods to the genre episodes and gazes ahead to where the series is going, this is a not-to-be-missed collection for the true fan.

Creating the Show

Show creator Andrew Marlowe explains:

> One of the reasons I wanted to do something like *Castle* is that I had grown up a fan of murder mysteries, not police procedurals. The ones on air – the *CSI*s and *Law & Order*s – approached subjects very darkly. I've always been a fan of shows like *Moonlighting* and thought taking that [murder mystery concept] and putting it in a [romantic] sparks-fly arena could be a lot of fun. ABC, a female-friendly network, seemed to be the right place – the Beckett character is a very strong woman – and *Castle* represents the different aspects of what it means to be a man: the long-suffering son of his mother, the incredibly kind and supportive dad, the rogue in relationships with women. (Ng, "Castle Creator")

Early in the process, goofy fan favorite Nathan Fillion joined up. Many have noted that with the toys and pop culture references, he *is* Castle. Fillion adds that while doing *Desperate Housewives*, he was handed a stack of scripts including the *Castle* pilot. Fifteen pages into it, he stopped reading and said to his girlfriend, "You tell me if you don't think this would be a lot of fun to do." (Ng, "Castle Creator"). Marlowe adds:

> I had been a Nathan Fillion fan for a long time – loved his work on *Firefly* and *Buffy the Vampire Slayer*. It seemed like the roles he was getting showcased one side of his talent, and I thought this would showcase everything he could do: the dramatic and the comedic. (Ng, "Castle Creator")

Now they needed a Beckett. This search took longer, with about 125 actresses trying out. In the first episode's commentary, Marlowe describes the purposeful way Stana Katic walked into auditions, and how she had enough muscle to take on Castle. Marlowe adds:

> Right when the 123rd actress walked into the room, you could see his eyes going like pinwheels. But when Stana walked in and they started saying the words, it became more electric. We had our fingers crossed that we had captured lightning in a bottle. (Ng, "Castle Creator")

They sold the pilot and the show was off.

The Plot Arcs

Beckett's Mother

Montgomery tells Castle of his first time meeting Beckett:

> I was working late one night, went down to archives to locate some old reports, and there she was with a flashlight and a banker's box open on her lap, studying this unsolved. She was a patrol cop then, she wasn't even authorized to be down there. When I asked her what the hell she was doing, she told me this was her mother's case.

He adds that he knew he couldn't do anything to stop her ("Knockout," 324). Indeed, Castle discovers in the first episode that her mother's unsolved murder has always driven Beckett. Johanna, a lawyer, was found stabbed in an alley, with her murder reported as a mugging gone wrong, and quietly dismissed.

Castle soon gets interested in solving the crime himself. However, Beckett resists. She tells him she isn't interested in opening the case again for the "same reason a recovering alcoholic doesn't drink." She adds:

> You don't think I haven't been down there? You don't think I haven't memorized every line in that file? My first three years on the force, every off-duty moment was spent looking for something someone missed. It took me a year of therapy to realize if I didn't let it go, it was gonna destroy me. And so I let it go. ("A Death in the Family," 110)

Castle begins digging into the case and they fight over his boundaries, causing a rift at the beginning of season two. He does discover that the killer murdered several people connected with Beckett's mother (a former law student of hers, a documents clerk and a lawyer for a non-profit), making this a series of targeted hits, not a mugging. The ME might have buried it, or might have been incompetent. He died four years earlier.

The first real lead shows up while investigating a mob hit in "Sucker Punch" (213).

> **Murray:** I used homographic reconstruction of Coonan's wounds to generate a 3D model of the blade used. It's a special operations group knife, the kind favoured by special forces in Gulf War One. He kills with a single blow, using these other wounds to camouflage the skill with which the initial stroke was delivered. The very same method and the very same weapon that the killer employed ten years ago.
> **Beckett:** Lanie?
> **Lanie:** I'm so sorry.
> **Murray:** Detective Beckett, there is no doubt in my mind that Jack Coonan was killed by the same man who murdered your mother. ("Sucker Punch," 213)

Beckett bargains to get her hands on the contract killer, Rathborne. However, Jack Coonan's brother Dick is the real killer – he claims it was Rathborne so he can get immunity. On Beckett's confronting him and demanding the man who hired him, Coonan snarks, "Forget it, you'll never touch him, he'll bury you" ("Sucker Punch," 213). He takes Castle hostage, and she's forced to shoot Coonan. To her despair, he dies. After, Castle comes and apologizes to Beckett.

> **Castle:** I overstepped. I came down here to say that I was sorry, and that I'm through. I can't shadow you anymore. If it wasn't for me...
> **Beckett:** If it wasn't for you I would have never found my mom's killer and someday soon I'm gonna find the sons of bitches who had Coonan kill her and I'd like you around when I do. And if you tell anyone what I'm about to say, there's gonna be another shooting, but – I've gotten used to you pulling my pigtails. I've a hard job,

Castle, and having you around makes it a little more
fun.
Castle: Your secret's safe with me. ("Sucker Punch,"
213)

She catches a break in "Knockdown" (313) when the
original detective on the case, John Raglan, calls for a
meeting. He confesses his past to her, explaining, "You
need some context here. This thing started about nineteen
years ago, back before I even knew who Johanna Beckett
was. Nineteen years ago I made a bad mistake. And that
started the dominoes falling, and one of them was your
mother." He adds that he was ordered to report the death
as random gang violence, but is killed by a sniper before
he can say more.

Investigating Raglan reveals he used to cover for
murders by the druglord Vulcan Simmons. Castle also
finds that Beckett's mother was researching the alley
where she was later killed.

Castle: Turns out before your mother there was another
murder in this alley, back when it was the back entrance
to a club called Sons of Palermo, it was an old Mafia
hang out.
Beckett: I didn't know this was a club.
Castle: Well it got shut down years before your mother
was killed, after an FBI agent by the name of Bob
Armund was killed in the alley behind it.
Beckett: It says Armund was working undercover in the
Mafia.
Castle: Somehow the mob got onto Armund, used the
old family remedy.
Beckett: Summary execution. NYPD arrested a mob
enforcer for Armund's murder, a guy by the name of Joe
Pulgatti. He later plead guilty, and guess who the
arresting officer was? Officer John Raglan.
("Knockdown," 313)

Pulgati tells a different story, of police officers
kidnapping mobsters and holding them for ransom. He
adds that Johanna Beckett was the only lawyer to believe

him and follow up on this case. He finishes, "She came to visit me here she said she'd look into my case, later I found out she was murdered. Don't get yourself killed chasing this thing. Take it from me, there's nothing more dangerous out there than a killer with a badge."

> **Castle**: They mistakenly killed an undercover fed named Bob Armund. To cover their asses they pinned Armund's murder on Pulgatti.
> **Beckett**: And then seven years later my mom and a group of her colleagues tried to put together an appeal for Pulgatti. Now the cops knew that if the case got over turned they would all be exposed . So they hired Dick Coonan to kill all of them.
> **Montgomery**: And Raglan wrote off their homicides as random gang violence.
> **Castle**: And that would have been the end of it, but Raglan found out he was dying said he wanted to come clean. So they had to silence him too.
> **Beckett**: Pulgatti said that there were three kidnappers in that van, that means there's at least two conspirators out there now.
> **Ryan**: And we already know who one of them is, Raglan's old academy buddy Gary McCallister.
> ("Knockdown," 313)

This man, McCallister, tells Beckett, "You want me to tell you about Joe Pulgatti? About the people he put in the hospital, the ones he put in the river? Me and the rest of those jackals fed him the city for decades. But you couldn't touch them because they brought everybody. This part, this part I want to you know, cause this part I'm not ashamed of, at least we tried to do something. It wasn't pretty and it wasn't legal, but it was right." He finishes by adding, as everyone else does, that the man who's been killing everyone as a cover-up is very powerful, someone Beckett can never touch. She ends the episode by arresting the sniper, Hal Lockwood (or so he calls himself), and telling him she'll come to prison every week until he tells her who hired him.

In the third season finale, Lockwood is "accidentally"

taken from segregation and he kills McCallister. Then fake cops free Lockwood during his arraignment. Castle realizes the next target is the third cop. This is in fact Montgomery, whom Lockwood commands to lure Beckett into a trap or his family will die. He sends seven missing police files to someone, and then Montgomery decoys Beckett to a hanger.

> **Beckett**: Give me a name. You owe me that, Roy.
> **Montgomery:** No, Kate. I give you a name, I know you. You'll run straight at him. I might as well shoot you where you stand.
> **Beckett**: That's why you brought me here, isn't it? To kill me?
> **Montgomery:** No, I brought you here to lure them.
> **Beckett**: You baited them?
> **Montgomery:** And now they're coming. I need you to leave. They're coming to kill you and I'm not going to let them. I'm going to end this. ("Knockout," 324)

He shoots the thugs and wounds Lockwood, and then warns Lockwood that Beckett is protected. Lockwood kills him. At his funeral, a sniper shoots Beckett, nearly fatally.

When she recovers, she finds the new Captain Gates has closed the investigation and her friends have been keeping their tiny leads secret. Beckett brings Castle back in and chases down every lead, as they grow increasingly futile. Then Castle gets a mysterious phone call.

> **Castle**: He's a friend of Montgomery's. Said he owed Montgomery his life. He said Montgomery sent him some files, files that if they ever got out, could hurt some very powerful people. They were using those files as a threat to keep Montgomery's family from ever being harmed. Beckett's safety was also part of the deal.
> **Martha:** But they went after her anyway.
> **Castle**: He didn't get the files until after she was shot. He says she's safe now, on one condition. She can't go

> near the case. If she does, he can't guarantee her
> safety. If she digs, they will kill her. ("Rise," 401)

He decides he'll need to be her partner again to steer her away from the case and protect her.

During season four, the shadowy figure continues contacting Castle. When the mayor is implicated, the shadowy figure offers advice. After they catch the criminal, a slippery lawyer arrives, suggesting he's protected from above ("Dial M for Mayor," 412).

At season end, Beckett gets another lead. A dead man was burgling Roy Montgomery's house, stealing his files and even wedding album in an attempt to identify someone. The man was killed by the same assassin that shot Beckett. Ryan insists they should tell Gates everything, but Esposito wants to leave it up to Beckett. Castle is finally forced to tell Beckett the truth:

> **Castle**: Before Montgomery went into that hangar, he
> sent a package to someone, someone...he trusted. It
> contained information damaging to the person behind all
> this. Montgomery was trying to protect you. But the
> package didn't arrive until after you'd been shot.
> Montgomery's friend struck a deal with them. If they left
> you alone, the package and the information inside
> would never see the light of day. But they made one
> condition – you had to back off. And that's the reason
> you are alive, Kate, because you stopped.
> **Beckett**: How do you know this?
> **Castle**: In order for the deal to work, someone had to
> make sure you weren't pursuing it.
> ...
> **Castle**: You keep going with this. They're gonna decide.
> They're gonna come for you Kate.
> **Beckett**: Let them come. They sent Coonan and he's
> dead. They sent Lockwood and he's dead. And I am still
> here, Castle. And I am ready.
> **Castle**: Ready for what. To-To die for your cause? This
> isn't a murder investigation anymore, Kate. They've
> turned it into a war.
> **Beckett**: If they want a war, then I will bring them a war,
> straight to their doorsteps.

> **Castle**: Well, I guess there's just nothing I can say is there?... Okay. Um. Yeah, You're right Kate. It's your life. You can throw it away if you want to, but I'm not gonna stick around to watch you. So, this is, uh, over. I'm done. ("Always," 423)

She keeps going and tracks down the assassin, Maddox. In the scuffle, Beckett is nearly killed and he escapes. At episode end, Maddox finds the mysterious man who's been keeping Beckett safe. He says, "What you had was blackmail. Now, you're going to tell me where all that information is. And after you do, I'm going to put Kate Beckett in the ground once and for all."

As season five starts, the team discovers what's happened. Castle tells Beckett, "Whatever information Montgomery gave to him, he's been using it to protect you. But now they've sent Maddox to hunt him down and get it back. If we don't get to him before Maddox does you'll never be safe again" ("After the Storm," 501). They find Michael Smith, tortured, with his blackmail file burned. However as they send him to the hospital, he mumbles part of an address. There, Beckett and Castle find another copy of the file.

Maddox sets a bomb, killing himself and destroying the papers, but they manage to save some scraps. Piecing them together, they find the man who orchestrated it all – William Bracken, now a US senator. Castle adds, "Well this would explain why he's coming after you right now. Word is, Bracken's being groomed to run for President." Beckett goes to his political event and confronts him in person, gun ready.

> **Beckett**: Roy Montgomery, McAllister, John Raglan, my mother. Everyone that you've ever had killed, I want you to admit to it.
> **Bracken:** Your mother's death was a tragedy. And I am deeply sorry for your loss. But I can't give you what you want.
> ...

Beckett: (low) Who do you think you're talking to? How can you justify yourself to me? My mother was stabbed, in an alley, because of you. She bled to death, alone, in a pile of garbage, so save me your campaign speeches about the great things!

Bracken: You sound a bit delusional, you know? But then again, who are you? You're a disgraced cop obsessed with her mother's murder. And who am I? I'm a decent man looking out for the little guy. That's who the public sees. And every time they elect me, I'm humbled. I strive harder to live up to that ideal, I want to be that man. And I won't let you or anyone else get in my way.

Beckett: I don't think you're in a position to threaten, Senator.

Bracken: See, here's what you don't understand. It's not who has the gun. It's who has the power. Do you really think that's you?

Beckett: I have the file. Smith had another copy. 0862241, that's the number of the bank account where you deposited the money orders. So you're right. It is about who holds the power. Now I could release that file and destroy you, but what would that mean for my life expectancy? So here's how it is. The deal that you had with Smith, that's our deal now. And if anything happens to me, or anyone that I care about, that file goes public. Am I clear? That's a yes or no question.

Bracken: (quietly) Yes.

Beckett: And one more thing. Whoever it is you think I am, whatever it is you think you know about me, you have no idea what I'm capable of or how far I will go. I am done being afraid. It's your turn now.

She raises her gun and pistol whips him with the side of it.

Beckett: That's gonna leave a nasty scar. Every time you see it think of me. ("After the Storm," 501)

At last she has his identity and has pushed back, though she has no way to arrest him yet. She continues watching and waiting, as well as sending his a threatening anonymous letter. As Bracken's actor adds:

Beckett and Bracken are so inexplicably linked. This is her quest, to get to this guy and bring him down. When

18

you have that kind of obsession, it colors all areas of your life. It affects your relationship, it affects your ability to work, it affects your ability to sleep. That's been going on for a long time with her. When you get to see them actually locking horns for a number of scenes, you realize how intense that kind of obsession is. (Ng, "*Castle*'s Jack Coleman")

In "Recoil" (513), the team discovers that someone plans to shoot Senator Bracken at an Eco Conference while he delivers his keynote speech. To Beckett's misery, she's assigned to lead the taskforce protecting him. "I was finally going to put this guy away, Castle. And now I'm protecting the man who killed my mother," she says. Beckett's hatred is so deep that the usual interrogation holds much more depth than usual. "She despises Bracken and loathes him," his actor says, "but because she's obsessed with bringing down this guy, everything is so loaded." (Ng, "*Castle*'s Jack Coleman")

> **Bracken:** Well. Hard to miss the irony of this situation.
> **Beckett:** (dryly) Senator Bracken, do you have any enemies? Is there anyone you can think of that would like to kill you?
> **Bracken:** I get threatening letters and emails all the time. Comes with the office. My chief of staff keeps a file.
> **Beckett:** Anyone with a legitimate claim?
> **Bracken:** A man doesn't get to my position without upsetting people along the way. Most of them aren't crazy enough to want to kill me. (he gestures) Present company excluded.
> **Beckett:** You know Senator, I'm not the one you should be worried about right now.
> **Bracken:** It's just us here, Detective. A shooter on the loose, me in the crosshairs. Must be a dream come true for you.
> **Beckett:** In my dreams I'm the one that gets to pull the trigger. But you know, if you're not comfortable with me leading this investigation you're welcome to step outside and tell everyone why. (silence) Well then, I guess we're stuck with each other. So then let me make one thing clear. This man killed Melanie Rogers. And when

> someone commits murder, whoever he is Senator, I will
> bring him to justice. No matter how long it takes.

Beckett finds a death threat letter, likely from the culprit, but considers throwing it away rather than using it to stop the assassin. Her psychologist tells her, "Maybe the right choice is the one you can live with." She does her duty, but can't bear to shoot a man whose claim to revenge is as legitimate as hers. In the end, she actually stakes her reputation on saving Bracken. He ends the episode owing her a favor.

In "In the Belly of the Beast" (617), Beckett is called on to impersonate a killer for hire and infiltrate a drug ring. Lazarus is their leader. Inside, she spies Vulcan Simmons directing the operation. He sentences her to die. However, the real killer for hire finds her and saves her. She tells Beckett that the mysterious Lazarus "sent me because he owed you. He said he wanted you to live." Beckett realizes there was someone behind Simmons and discovers the drug money was going to Future Forward, a political Super PAC...run by Bracken. He's making a run for the White House.

As season six comes to a close, on her own time, Beckett is investigating drug lord Vulcan Simmons and DC political consultant Jason Marks when the latter is mysteriously killed.

> **Beckett**: Six weeks, Castle. Six weeks following Vulcan
> Simmons, hoping for a lead. And when we finally find
> someone that connects him to Bracken the guy ends up
> dead in an alley?
> **Castle:** If Jason Marks is the conduit between Vulcan's
> drug money and Senator Bracken's presidential
> campaign, why would they kill him?
> **Beckett**: Something's changed. Maybe Bracken's
> firewalling himself again. Erasing all of the dots before
> they connect back to him. We have to move fast, before
> those dots disappear. ("Veritas," 622)

Then Vulcan Simmons is found tortured and executed with Beckett's gun. Smith is seen prowling around and the cops wonder if he faked his own death. But worse, Beckett is a target once more. As she notes:

> Bracken knows that I was bluffing now. That I don't have this huge file of evidence against him. Because if I did I wouldn't have to go after Vulcan to bring him down. I've overplayed my hand. There's nothing to stop him from killing me anymore, so...he's making his move. And I have to make mine.

Smith meets them in the parking garage and tells them, "I got to one of Bracken's men, who told me there was something that the Senator was afraid of. A recording made by a former associate to protect himself. A recording in which Bracken admits to murder." Smith was working with Jason Marks on this before he was suddenly killed.

Back at the precinct, Esposito and Ryan bring Gates into their conspiracy at last. Castle and Beckett go on the run, but Bracken catches Beckett alone and orders his men to drug her and make her appear to commit suicide. She outwits them and kills them before collapsing.

While asleep, Kate has a dream-flashback of Montgomery urging her to search her mother's things for the tape and realizes it really does exist and that Montgomery must have made it and given it to her mother. She and Castle go back and search her mother's things, but the only significant clue appears when Castle reads her datebook entry "D Me w/Family" not as "dinner with family" but as "Detective Montgomery evidence with family." The family is the group of elephants on Beckett's desk, and she dramatically opens it and finds the tape just as she's put under arrest. Cleared, she arrests Bracken and the conspiracy is ended at last.

Beckett's Trainer

Mike Royce, who visits in "Under the Gun" (303), was one of Beckett's first mentors. She tells him, "I was drowning, and... you were dry land. All they ever taught us in the academy was how to do paperwork. You were the one who taught me how to be a cop." He also knows humorous stories about her past, including a karaoke stakeout, as he describes a time Beckett offered to show a criminal the guy her boobs if he dropped his speargun.

He's now a bounty hunter and joins in their case. When she discovers he was only using them to find a buried treasure, she sadly tells him over the phone that she was in love with him. As she adds:

> You were the only one who understood the obsession that drove me, who didn't tell me that I would get over my mother's murder and that she wouldn't want me to do this...I dreamt about you. The night that I shot the guy who killed my mother, I dreamt that I was the one who was on the ground dying, and that you came up to me and told me to stand up, 'cause there was still work to be done. When I woke up that morning, I just wanted to call you, but we hadn't talked in so long.

However, she reveals to the team that she only said all this to stall him while they traced his call. As she concludes to him, "I'm going to catch Carver's killer, Royce. And then I'm going to recover Lloyd's score. And when I arrest you, you're gonna realize that what you destroyed today was worth a hell of a lot more than money." She reluctantly arrests him at episode end, which he accepts philosophically.

Upon his release, he loses his bounty hunter license and relocates to Los Angeles. There, he stays in Gene Simmons' guest house after helping the rock star. In fact, Royce becomes a "trouble-shooter," fixing people's problems. However, when Royce's latest client is tricked into stealing a new type of dissolving bullet, Royce is killed by industrial thief Russell Ganz. .

22

Beckett pursues the criminal to L.A., against orders. Castle, of course, goes with her.

> **Ganz:** I knew you were a cop.
> **Beckett:** My name is Detective Kate Beckett, NYPD. Michael Royce was my friend. You shot him and left him in an alley like a piece of garbage. Consider this poetic justice.
> **Ganz:** He said something about hell raining down on me. I never imagined hell looked like you. ("To Love and Die in L.A.," 322)

Despite her anger, she takes him down only to turn him over to local police.

At episode end, Beckett discovers Royce's last words in a letter to her. He writes:

> And now for the hard part, kid. It's clear that you and Castle have something real. And you're fighting it. But trust me, putting the job ahead of your heart is a mistake. Risking our hearts is why we're alive. The last thing you want is to look back on your life and wonder, 'if only'" ("To Love and Die in L.A.," 322)

3XK

The Triple Killer, or "3XK," is a serial killer who would kill three blonde women in a week by strangulation, leaving them in their own apartments, hands clasped peacefully. After a month, he would begin killing again. April 23-29, 2006, and May 7-13, 2006, he killed six women, entering their apartments through disguises like security guard or cable repairman.

The episode "3XK" (306) marks the murderer's return. Captain Montgomery, who was on the original task force, is determined to capture him. Castle is also an expert, as he studied the killer for his novel *When It Comes to Slaughter*.

Linda Russo, the new victim, originally called the police about a creepy cable repairman and thus was instrumental in stopping 3XK, who went into hiding. She is killed outside, likely because she wouldn't have let 3XK into her building.

The team suspects Marcus Gates, recently released from prison, and talks with his cellmate Jerry Tyson (Michael Mosley) about his habits. While they find Marcus and question him, he remains very cool, knowing they don't have enough to hold him, and he walks out the front door. Jerry cuts a deal and is released from prison. They find Marcus trying to kill Jerry's girlfriend Donna, and Marcus confesses to all eight murders in exchange for his partner Paul getting full immunity. The case is closed.

Castle and Ryan go to see Jerry Tyson and give him the news. However, when Jerry doesn't ask about his supposed girlfriend, Castle realizes something is wrong – Jerry Tyson is the real killer. He has paid for Paul's expensive operation in return for Marcus taking the blame, leaving Tyson free to kill again. Tyson knocks them out, ties them up, and steals Ryan's gun. Helpless otherwise, Castle takes him on verbally:

> **Castle**: Oh, it's really not complicated. You were raised by a single mother. She was blonde, she was beautiful, but she never wanted you. When you were, what, twelve? She died, suddenly. Let's say drug overdose. You went foster care, the bad kind. You've so much hate. So much hate towards your mother for abandoning you that you kill these women to get back at her. But you leave them looking peaceful because as much as you hated your mother, you loved your mother. Am I getting warm?
> **Jerry**: You're drawn to death. You like to be around it, because it thrills you. Now, where does that come from? Your own suppressed impulses? *[Leans forward]* How close to death do you want to get, huh? ("3XK," 306)

After their showdown, Tyson escapes.

> **Beckett**: Tell me something, Castle. Why did he let you live?

24

> **Castle**: To punish me. Make me pay for ruining his plan.
> Now he's going to kill again, all because I couldn't stop
> him. And I feel so...
> **Beckett**: I know the feeling.
> **Castle**: I know you do. ("3XK," 306)

In season four, Ryan's weapon appears as Tyson gave
it to Philip Lee, an enemy from prison, to mess with Lee
as well as the police. When the enemy kills a young
woman, Ryan is distraught:

> **Castle**: You know, Ryan, none of this is your fault. The
> fact that he used your gun...
> **Kevin Ryan**: That weapon was issued to me by the city
> of New York. I let it out of my hand, and now a girl is
> dead. So please do not tell me that it's not my fault.
> ("Kick the Ballistics," 404)

Lee tries to cut a deal for information about Tyson,
but Castle believes any details he knows on Tyson will be
faked:

> **Beckett**: So, Lee wants 15 to 25 with parole in 10 for
> giving us Tyson's new alias and I need to give the DA a
> recommendation. This might be our chance to get 3XK,
> Castle.
> **Castle**: No. (he levels a look) It's a setup. Jerry Tyson
> gave the gun to Phillip Lee knowing that he would use it,
> so there's a good chance we knew he'd eventually get
> to Phillip.
> **Beckett**: Maybe. So what?
> **Castle**: So nothing Tyson told Phillip would be the truth.
> Giving Phillip a good deal for bad information...that's
> just another win for Jerry Tyson.
> **Beckett**: Are you sure?
> **Castle**: Sure enough. Jane Herzfeld deserves justice.
> Life in prison for Phillip Lee. No deals. We'll get 3XK.
> And we'll do it right. ("Kick the Ballistics," 404)

Lee gets no deal. Captain Gates states that they will "track
down Jerry Tyson like the animal he is, and haul him into
custody" ("Kick the Ballistics," 404)

"Probable Cause" (505) begins with a grisly ritualistic murder, and Castle's prints found at the scene. As they discover the victim had a secret boyfriend and find Castle on camera buying her jewelry, they arrest him. A deleted file in his hard drive that perfectly describes the murder and the tools used to kill her are found in his loft. Castle and Beckett are stunned by this development, until Tyson sneaks into lockup to reveal to Castle that he is the real culprit. Desperate, Castle escapes custody before Tyson can have him killed. The team struggle to prove 3XK was involved. At last, Tyson attacks Castle and Beckett. While Tyson holds Beckett at gunpoint on a bridge, Castle shoots him and he falls into the water. When the body can't be found, Castle suspects Tyson is still out there.

In the sixth season's "Disciple" (609), two bodies appear that resemble Lanie and Esposito. It turns out the victims have been surgically altered by Doctor Kelly Nieman (Annie Wersching), Tyson's girlfriend, to look this way. Castle wonders if these terribly personal murders are the work of 3XK, but they discover all his files were checked out by "Esposito" while the medical results and DNA were removed by "Lanie." All evidence to connect Jerry Tyson to his crimes is gone. "It's not enough that Jerry Tyson disappeared, he wanted his murders to disappear, too. And it's not just evidence. It's his MOs, his victim preferences. All the hundreds of tiny case details that could reveal psychology as to where he is, where he might be going next. It's all gone. It's like he's got a clean slate," Castle says. At episode end, they find a USB embedded in a pen that plays the song "We'll Meet Again."

Doctor Kelly Nieman begins giving women plastic surgery to look more like Tyson's preferred victims, who in turn resemble his blonde foster mother. Castle and Beckett arrest him, but are unable to prove he's Tyson, as he claims he's Mike Boudreau and has had plastic surgery to *look* like the serial killer. While he's being interrogated, his partner kidnaps Beckett ("Resurrection," 714).

Castle chases him down alone, only to walk into Tyson's trap – Beckett is being held far away and each must watch the other suffer. However, Castle reveals this was *his* set-up: he knew that the only way to find Tyson and Beckett was to let Tyson kidnap him. "I let you bring me here. It was the only way to find you. I needed to find you so I could find her. But the truth, Jerry?...The truth is, I lured you here. To watch you die." Castle had an earpiece the whole time connecting him to the team. He tells Esposito to take the shot, and Tyson dies at last. They charge in to save Beckett only to find Beckett has saved herself and killed Nieman. It's over ("Reckoning, 715).

Castle's Father and the CIA

> **Alexis:** It's like... I have this family tree, and there's a whole chunk of it missing. There's a whole part of my history that doesn't even exist. I mean, really, how could gram not know?
> **Castle:** My first year of college, I, uh, went to a party, met this girl – Allison. In the space of six hours, we met, we talked, we danced, we fell in love. The next morning, she was gone. I spent a year trying to find her, but I never learned her last name. There's not a week that goes by I don't think about her. Your gram told me that she loved a lifetime the night she met him.
> **Alexis:** Don't you feel like you're missing out, not knowing?
> **Castle:** No. Oh, no. That's the beauty of the mystery. Right now, my father could be an astronaut, a pirate, a humanitarian, winner of the Nobel prize. I mean, what one man could live up to all that? ("Suicide Squeeze," 215)

In "Fool Me Once" (204) Castle tells Beckett he has a contact in the CIA. This in fact is serious foreshadowing for later. At the start of "Pandora" (415) Thomas Gage hurls a man out a window then takes a hostage. When the NYPD arrest him, he tells them he and all the evidence will disappear…then they do.

> **Lanie:** The man doesn't exist as far as I can tell.
> **Beckett:** So you haven't ID'd him yet?
> **Lanie:** Look, I'm trying. But his fingerprints aren't in any database, which is weird because I thought for sure he'd have a criminal record.
> **Castle:** How come?
> **Lanie:** It's not the first time this guy's mixed it up. Old gunshot wounds, calloused hands from martial arts training. More broken bones than Evel Knievel. You're not going to believe his x-rays.

On the case, Beckett and Castle suddenly get bags thrust over their heads. They emerge in a set of offices, all cool blues and metal and high tech, and are dragged far far down in an elevator.

> **Beckett:** What is this place?
> **Castle:** Uh…uh…I don't know. I have no idea.
> **Sophia Turner:** Rick Castle as a loss for words? That must be a first for you.
> **Castle:** Sophia Turner.
> **Sophia Turner:** Hello, Rick. Welcome to the CIA.

As Sophia gradually reveals, she was Castle's muse (and lover) about twelve years before. As Sophia explains to Beckett, "Rick and I met when he was just beginning to do research on his first Derrick Storm novel. He wanted an up close and personal look at the life of a female CIA agent. So I gave him one."

As Beckett realizes, "You're Clara Strike? The Clara Strike from the Derrick Storm books?" She's gorgeous and flirtatious enough that Beckett is jealous of the muse part. Meanwhile, Gage has gone rogue and is trying to create a catastrophe. With her hands tied on US soil, Sophia asks Castle and Beckett to investigate: "Thomas Gage is a hired gun. We don't know who he works for or how deep this goes. All I am asking is that you continue your investigation and we will share all information we get on him."

Castle eagerly accepts the assignment, not only to serve his country and help his old girlfriend but to "play spy." Throwing himself into the role, he teases Ryan and Esposito:

> **Castle:** No. Hey, sorry boys. Classified. Top secret. Our eyes only, def-com one. And if I did tell you? Well then, I'd have to kill you.
> **Esposito:** Yeah? Good luck with that.

Castle and Beckett discover that a professor has discovered a weakness in US security, a linchpin that was tied to the US economy that would cause a monumental crisis. Now the Eastern Europeans have his plan and will use it to cause World War III ("Linchpin," 416). Gage appears to be a mole for the bad guys, but he reveals he's still loyal and has only been used as a diversion. The mole hunt goes on through the story – a popular CIA plot.

> **Sophia Turner:** So you think there's someone in the CIA? A mole, a traitor. Is that what you think? You know, I think you could be right. And I think it's you.
> **Gage:** You're making a mistake.

Sophia is finally revealed as the real mole, and reveals a secret of her own:

> **Sophia Turner:** I'll just tell them how we all tried to stop it and couldn't and the two of you were killed in the process, by Danberg, of course. Don't worry. I'll make it sound heroic. Your father would be very proud.
> **Castle:** My father?
> **Sophia Turner:** You don't think you gained special access to the CIA back then because of your charm. You really don't know, do you? I guess you never will.

She's killed moments later, leaving Castle to puzzle over all she's said.

In season five, kidnappers take Alexis and her college

friend, a dignitary's daughter. The other girl's family pays the ransom, but Alexis isn't released. Castle flies to Paris to pay serious men to track her down illegally. When he goes to exchange several million dollars cash for her in the Forest of Fontainebleau, he discovers that Henri, the man he hired, has set him up and plans to murder him and take the money. To Castle's confusion, Henri says, "I value my life more than my word. If I had known who was really holding your daughter, who your daughter really is – ("Hunt," 516). Castle of course has no idea what the man means. Suddenly another man all in black shoots Henri then beckons Castle to get in his car. He identifies himself as Jackson Hunt.

> **Castle:** Sounds made up.
> **Hunt:** (smirks) It is.

Castle realizes this man has been tracking their suspects and torturing them. Given his dwindling options, he goes with Hunt, who points out he could have killed Castle several times over and insists he's one of the good guys. When they go to Hunt's safehouse, Castle sees a collection of photos of Alexis there. Then he gets a call:

> **Castle:** It's not Beckett. It's a local number. (he realizes) Alexis. (he picks up) Alexis?
> **Volkov:** I'm afraid not, Mr. Castle. But I am the one holding her. If you value her life you will give the phone to the man standing next to you. The one responsible for all the bloodshed in the woods.
> Castle is confused but does as instructed.
> **Hunt:** Yeah.
> **Volkov:** It's you. After all these years, it's finally you.
> **Hunt:** Time to let her go, Volkov.
> **Volkov:** The way you let Anna go? No. It's time to end things. A life for a life. Tomorrow, 6AM. Outside the Palais Le Bon. You show, I'll spare her. But if you don't I will put a bullet in her brain instead of yours. And we start again.

When Castle confusedly asks Hunt what's going on, the man replies that this is an operation meant to hurt him. "Because she is my granddaughter. Richard, I'm your father." He adds that he's a spy. "What I do means no communication, no relationships, to anyone. But, hey, I've been around. We've met before. Yeah. When you were about ten years old." At the library he gave Castle a copy of *Casino Royale,* which made him want to be a writer. Hunt adds, "I greased some wheels at the CIA when you were trying to get access to some information for research. I know that's not much, but for a minute there it made me feel like a father. No, I've been checking on you, and your mom, and Alexis your whole lives."

Now Gregor Volkov. KGB's most feared agent, wants revenge. Hunt tells Castle, "You've been playing cop for years. Ready to play spy?" Coordinating their efforts, they trick Volkov and save Alexis. Hunt adds that he will vanish forever. Perhaps someday they will have time to be a family, but not yet. He insists that he can't even tell Castle if he survives, "Not officially, at least." As Hunt adds, "I know this has been tough for you, Richard, and I just want you to know, son...I've always been proud of you. Always." Back home Castle receives a copy of *Casino Royale* in the mail, alerting him that his father indeed survived.

Investigating a hacker's murder a year later, Castle receives a call: "Richard, something is about to happen. But you cannot react," the voice tells him ("Deep Cover," 612). Anderson Cross, head of the hacked company Universal Banking Solutions, is actually Castle's mysterious father. They meet after, in the park.

> **Castle:** I never thought I'd see you again.
> **Cross:** Ted Rollins, your victim. What have you learned?
> **Castle:** (scoffs) What have I learned? I'm sorry, until a year ago I had no idea who you were and now you come out of the blue and the only thing you have to say

is 'what have you learned'? How about 'hello son.
How've you been?'
Cross: You're getting emotional. Now's not the time.
Castle: Really? (he checks his watch) Because it's
been about 40 years, so when would be a good time?
Cross: With what I do? Never. Or did you forget what
happened in Paris?
Castle: No. How could I forget?
Cross: Then stop acting like you did. You know what I
do, you know who I am. I let my guard down, people
die.

Cross, who appears to have committed the murder, vanishes along with his company. To Castle's shock, Beckett identifies him as a *former* CIA operative. "He was disowned for an unauthorized assassination. He was sentenced to life, broke out, killed three guys in the process. This guy's wanted by our government. Now my friend said the rumor is he's working as a hitman." Castle discusses the situation with his mother, wondering whether his father lied, when his father arrives at the door, shot. Castle and Martha tend his wound. He tells Castle, "I work outside the system, which means I needed an effective cover. Hired assassin, wanted by Uncle Sam? Opens a lot of doors." After Beckett arrives, he goes on to explain that the murdered hacker was working for him. "There was a massive breach at the CIA. Someone hacked the files containing the identities of our deep operatives.... That's why they called me. Because I'm outside. My orders were to find the mole and recover the files."

The Iranian CIA has an exchange planned to buy the list at Central Library. Castle's father is injured, so Beckett and Castle volunteer to stop him. His father gives him a hug and thanks him. When all goes downhill, Castle's father arrives and shoots the bad guy, revealing that he slipped a tracer on Castle during the hug.

Castle: Blaine killed Ted but left his body at Coney
Island. It was my father that moved the body. Now he

could have put it anywhere, but he took it to Ted's
apartment. Now do you know why?
Beckett: To bring him into our jurisdiction.
Castle: He wanted us to catch the case so he could
work me for information.
Beckett: Well maybe he was just looking for a reason to
see you again and this was his way.
Castle: I keep making the mistake of thinking he's
family. But he's not. You are.

Another relative appears when Beckett is in danger in
season eight:

Rita: Get in.
Beckett: No. No. Not until you tell me who you are.
Rita: You can call me Rita. I'm Castle's stepmother.
Now, we really have to go.
…
Beckett: So, what are you? CIA?
Rita: Oh, god. No. I'm a different three-letter agency.
Much more exclusive. ("XX," 802)

Like Castle's father, she appears to want to protect
Castle and Beckett, though she's keeping many secrets.
She reveals that she and Castle's father rarely see each
other, as the price for their safety and anonymity. She
urges Beckett to go on the run as well, but aids her when
Beckett refuses. Both she and Hunt are still out there, on
dangerous missions as they keep the world safe.

Beckett and the FBI

Beckett and Castle team up with experienced FBI
Special Agent Jordan Shaw in the hunt for a serial killer.
Beckett is jealous of Castle's admiration for Shaw and the
FBI's hi-tech gadgets. Meanwhile, she and Shaw develop a
strong working relationship in a short time ("Tick Tick
Tick," 217).

In "The Human Factor" (523), Homeland Security
takes over their case, by the end, however, Agent Stack is
asking Beckett where her ambition lies and telling her, "I

used to work homicide, too.... 'til some guy tapped me on the shoulder. Today I'm that guy. What I'm saying is this. I think you're exceptional. You're smart. You're strong. You're an asymmetrical thinker. I see bigger things for you." He tells her there's a job opening in DC. "With the Attorney General. We report directly to him, we work with total autonomy on the biggest, most challenging cases. Cases like this. Where the stakes are high and the outcome can affect history. Not everybody has what it takes for the job. I think you do."

She thinks about it, and interviews in the next episode without telling Castle. As she confesses to her father, discussing it with Castle would mean they would have to make choices about the relationship...however, when she gets the job, she decides she truly wants it. Gates too encourages her to take it and use her talents to the utmost. At last, Castle proposes before hearing whether she got the job, insisting he wants to spend his life with her.

Two months later in DC, working with the Attorney General's office, she has to cancel her visit to New York once again. Castle flies in to surprise her, but when he follows her around her crime scene, Beckett's new partner Rachel McCord isn't amused. She tells Beckett, "Do you realize what would happen if I told the Chief that he was here? You would be kicked off the team" and adds to Castle, "Not to mention obstruction charges against you. This is my one and only warning. The next time I see you it better be on a book jacket" ("Valkyrie," 601). Though Castle keeps attempting to shadow Beckett, he soon realizes that they're no longer partners and he's not welcome in Federal investigations. Of course, before he can leave, he's infected with a deadly virus. With only 24 hours to live, Castle is allowed to work the case with them. At its end, however, he's bundled back to New York.

The third episode sees Beckett return to New York to investigate a Federal aspect of the latest murder ("Need to

VALERIE ESTELLE FRANKEL

Know," 603). This time, all her team are irritated at being kept in the dark with Beckett and McCord's insistence on "need to know." By case end, however, even Beckett is uncomfortable. A young Russian woman is pressured to spy on her family now that her boyfriend, the original spy, has been murdered.

> **Beckett:** The man that she loved was murdered and he's going to send her on a suicide mission?
> **McCord:** Like I said, we don't always see the whole picture.
> **Beckett:** I think this one's pretty clear.

Beckett releases a story to the media that blows Svetlana's cover and makes her useless as a spy. After, McCord appears at her door. "They know it was you that tipped off the press. A part of me really admires you for the choice that you made, maybe because I'd like to think there was a time that I would have done it. But the people we answer to don't feel that way…Kate, you're one of the best agents I've ever worked with. But I'm here to tell you you're fired." Within an episode, Beckett regains her old police job and returns to the precinct.

Beckett's Mother, Castle's Stepmother and the Next Conspiracy

Season eight picks up the threads of this plot as Beckett's old team are all suddenly killed offscreen. A survivor, Vikram Singh (Sunkrish Bala), contacts her. He tells her "This is an emergency alert, classification protocol seven," and she sneaks off to see him without telling Castle. He's being chased by assassins, and tells her, "Look, whoever these guys are, they are hacked in everywhere. Which means anybody you call is gonna wind up dead" ("XX," 802).

Vikram reveals that a two-year-old search Beckett performed on William Bracken finally got a hit. "The document it uncovered was a just-declassified Electronic

35

memo, heavily redacted. From what I could tell, it detailed a meeting between a federal official of some kind and Senator William Bracken" ("XX," 802). The word "loksat" is scribbled in the margin, along with an airplane number. Finding it unleashes a deadly protocol, and teams of assassins go after Beckett and Vikram. They also kill Senator Bracken in prison.

Castle's stepmother tells them they are in such danger they will need to flee the country and go into hiding to survive. She adds:

> What I do know is the person behind this is a very powerful and a very dirty analyst inside the CIA. I've been trying to get an identity for over a year, and every time I get a lead, it just evaporates. ...As you know, the senator was working with a drug dealer by the name of Vulcan Simmons. They were using the profits to fund Bracken's presidential campaign. I mean, you must have wondered how they got away with it for so long. They were protected by Bracken's mystery partner. They were using CIA resources to import the drugs into the country.

Beckett and Vikram both decide not to run, but to make themselves bait and arrest the hit squad. Castle and Beckett independently track down the plane, and finally present themselves as enough of a target that they capture the bad guys. However, Allison Hyde, the second in command from the Attorney General's office, who collects the criminals, is revealed as their handler. The conspiracy goes on...

Montreal

Castle vanishes just before his wedding when an SUV runs him off the road. For two months, Beckett searches, but the clues are disheartening – Castle himself appears to have paid to have the SUV torched and crushed, suggesting the kidnapping was at his design. After Beckett has nearly given up hope, Castle is discovered unconscious in a dingy at sea, surrounded by bullet holes. Back in the hospital, he wakes with amnesia ("Driven," 701).

As he and Beckett piece together clues through the first two episodes, they discover he was camping on a beach in the northeast, or so it appears. A local man reports this, then vanishes, revealing he was an imposter rather than the landowner.

Further, Castle discovers photos that place him in Montreal. There he finds a safety deposit box in which he left loving but vague messages for his family. When he tracks down the room where he recorded them, the imposter from the beach reappears. He tells Castle his darkest secret as proof that Castle insisted on forgetting what happened to him, and adds that he and his associates made sure to arrange this. Castle and Beckett are left in the dark ("Montreal," 702).

A glimpse of a ruthless mercenary triggers a recurring dream for Castle – a car chase and shots fired in Thailand, a man bleeding under his hands ("Sleeper," 720). Then flashes of an old acquaintance and a school trophy. Castle sees Beckett's therapist and tries hypnosis to remember the details. After, he recalls a debate trophy, but the man he won it with remembers nothing about being in Thailand...or even in debate. The license plate from the car chase leads them to Chiang Mai, a province in northern Thailand.

They find the CIA handler Castle recalls, only to find him dead in his apartment. Tracking his movements, Castle finds himself at a restaurant where he recognizes a busboy, his old schoolmate Bilal.

> **Bilal:** Look, after I left the intelligence service I lost my way. I joined Al-Qaida.
> **Castle:** You were in Al-Qaida?
> **Bilal:** Will you please keep your voice down? Yes, I was. I rose up to become part of the senior leadership.

Castle: And now you're bussing tables and you live here?
Bilal: I chose this life. It's my penance. I wanted to leave Al-Qaida and I had inside knowledge about that organization. So I struck a deal with American intelligence to trade what I knew for a second chance.

He defected, and needed the CIA to bring him in alongside someone he trusted, somebody too prominent to be eliminated. This was Castle. However, Bilal goes on the run once again.

At episode end, the fake Jenkins saves him from the mercenary, and Castle demands answers:

Castle: What? Are you going to kill me? You can't. Raise too many questions. That's why you brought me back from Thailand, minus my memory. I was gone two months, thanks to you. I missed my wedding. What couldn't wait one more day?
Jenkins: There was a ticking clock. We picked up chatter about a major Al-Qaida strike in the US. We knew it was hours away and there was never enough time for us to put the pieces together in order to stop it.
Castle: But Bilal knew about the strike.
Jenkins: Names, places, operational details. We were desperate for Bilal and his intel, and when his contact was killed we needed you to get Bilal. And he came through. We were able to prevent the strike and we neutralized everyone involved. That's all I can tell you. And I expect you not to repeat it. Think of it this way: yeah, you missed your wedding. But you also saved tens of thousands of lives.

As Castle adds at episode end, more questions linger: "Like, how did I get shot? Why was I gone for two months?" Thus the story is left open for another revelation.

Katic adds that season eight will tackle this further:

Part of the exciting thing about this season is the way Alexi and Terence have envisioned the cosmic version of why the two characters (Castle and Beckett) have come together, how did these roads combine. It delves into the mythology of Rick's disappearance and memory loss as well as into what inspired Beckett to become a cop in the first place. (Andreeva)

Senator Beckett

Beckett's time pursuing corrupt Senator Bracken and grimacing at his hypocrisy seems to affect her: The time traveler Simon Doyle gives Castle a glimpse of the future, quoting his book jackets as saying, "Richard Castle lives in New York with his wife, Senator Beckett, and their three children" ("Time Will Tell," 605).

This plot gets another nod at the end of season seven:

> **Beckett:** Backstabbing, adultery, and betrayal. That is why I hate politics. Representatives of the people should be honorable. They should be trustworthy.
> **Castle:** Oh, I'm sure some of them are. But Washington could probably use a few more people that think the way you do. (he sets the box on her desk and moves an envelope to find a copy of the NYPD Captain's Exam Tutorial) What's this?
> **Beckett:** Oh, study materials.
> **Castle:** For the captain's exam. So you're going to go for it?
> **Beckett:** Well, it's the next step. I'm not sure if it's the right one. Yet. But I figured I'd take the test, see how I do. ("At Close Range," 718)

Soon after, she's hauled into a performance review and criticized about every aspect of her life, every mistake she's made. However, as she starts to leave, she turns back.

> **Beckett:** You're wrong, sir!
> **Supervisor:** Excuse me?
> **Beckett:** I said "you're wrong." In every case you have referenced, I've not only successfully brought the killer to justice, but I did so with the utmost respect for the law and for the department I represent. And regarding my relationship with Mr. Castle, he has proven to be a brilliant partner, and he's always had my back. And as for his...fictional representation of me, I'm proud to have

been his inspiration, and I'm proud to be his wife! You asked, how do I expect to lead? By continuing to fight for what's right, not for what's easy. My job is to protect the citizens of New York, and I will do it by doing my job better than anyone else and getting results! I don't cross the line - I put myself on it! And if you have any other questions, then you can ask the families of the victims that I have served!

Supervisor 2: Detective Beckett, sit down! [She sits.] That was an impassioned and powerful response. In fact, that was exactly what we were hoping for.

Supervisor: This wasn't a performance review.

Beckett: Then why would you attack me like that?

Supervisor: We wanted to see if you can defend yourself. Kate, this was an audition.

Beckett: For what?

Supervisor 2: Your future! We were looking for someone like you, someone who is incorruptible, certifiable hero where the people can get behind. Kate, you're bigger than what you're doing now, you know it. It's why you went to D.C., it's why you took the captain's exam. You want a bigger station, we wanna give it to you. We think you have an amazing future.

Beckett: Doing what?

Supervisor: We'd like you to run for New York State Senate. ("Hollander's Woods," 724)

The actress's contract was being negotiated at the time. If Beckett had needed to leave the show she could of course have taken the job and left for D.C. In what might have been the final episode, Castle suggests that he could follow his muse and switch to writing political thrillers. All this, however, gets postponed for a time, as Beckett prefers becoming captain of her old precinct.

Terence Paul Winter, *Castle*'s new showrunner, said having Beckett run for office is "something we absolutely considered, and it's not like it's off the table." For the near future, however, Beckett won't be going down that road. Deciding Beckett's career path, "What we realized is that the best way to tell *Castle*'s stories is to have Castle investigating twisty, fun cases. And the best way to do that is to keep Beckett in the precinct" (Mitovich).

40

The Castle-Becket Romance

Stana Katic (Beckett): "I might be naively romantic, but I believe that a relationship can be just as spicy when people get together as it was in the chase. The complications that happen when characters like Beckett and Castle get together can make for interesting viewing. They have ex-boyfriends and ex-girlfriends, he has a certain kind of lifestyle and she has a certain kind of lifestyle – and then on top of all that, they actually really care for each other. It would be neat to see how these two people attract each other and drive each other crazy. I'd love to see what happens when Beckett actually touches on a couple of his pet peeves. It would be fun to see her torture him a little bit, you know, in a fun way." (Bierly et al.)

Nathan Fillion (Castle): "When you get people together, [viewers] stop with the yearning, they stop with the wanting. They go, 'Ah, finally. They're together. All right, what else is on?' I know as an audience member, I enjoy knowing more than the characters I watch on TV know. [With our show it's] looking at these two, saying, 'Just turn around! She's making the face right now! She's making the face! You'll see it! Ah, you missed it.' The lack of resolution is what keeps people coming back. I think the challenge is how do you serve that so it's not repetitive." (Bierly et al.)

Ryan: *[pointing to inscription on Castle's book]* From the library of Katherine Beckett.
Beckett: Do you have a problem with reading, Ryan?
Esposito: Yo, check it, girl, you're totally a fan!
Beckett: Right. Of the genre.
Ryan: Right, the genre, that's why you're blushing.
Beckett: What are you, twelve? ("Flowers for your Grave," 101)

Wolkowski: You're really basing your book on Detective Beckett?

Castle: Every artist needs a muse.
Beckett: Call me a muse one more time, and I'll break both your legs, 'kay? ("Hell Hath no Fury," 104)

Castle: You okay?
Beckett: Yeah. Why?
Castle: Can't be easy breaking that kind of news.
Beckett: Yeah. Well, thanks for not making it a joke.
Castle: Hey, I'm a wise-ass, not a jack-ass.
Beckett: I didn't know there was a difference. ("Hell Hath no Fury," 104)

Beckett: Castle, what are you doing?
Castle: Promise not to hate me?
Beckett: I already hate you. ("Hell Hath no Fury," 104)

Alexis: How's it going with Detective Beckett?
Castle: What do you mean?
Alexis: Oh, come on, dad, you are basing a character off her. And you always say you have to love your characters.
Castle: Well, she is a character. But, uh, it's just research, nothing more.
Alexis: Yeah, I'm sure. ("Hell Hath no Fury," 104)

"The way I've been approaching that whole situation is Beckett is this prude of a character, she's really hard to scratch the surface and get underneath to something deeper," Fillion said. "It took years and years to wear this woman down. She gets so dark and brooding and she's often angry and just short-tempered, and Castle just wears his joy on his sleeve. He's that kind of a man. He likes life. He loves people. So it would fit to reason that Beckett had all of this history and this crazy stuff going on that made her so tough, and here we have Castle, not so tough. He's an okay guy." (Highfill)

Castle brings Beckett coffee for the first time of many in "Little Girl Lost," (109). Her drink of choice is a grande skim latte, with two pumps of sugar free vanilla. Castle tells her after, "Most people come up against a wall, they give up. Not you. You don't let go. You don't back down. That's what makes you extraordinary" ("A Death in the Family," 110).

Every time they stumble into a supernatural mystery, Castle instantly believes – psychics, mummies, ghosts. He also spins far-fetched tales of bodysnatchers and CIA plots, often borrowed from his favorite movies. Beckett, by contrast, invariably insists on a rational explanation. Castle retorts on one occasion, "Oh, so you don't believe in fate, yet your 'gut' has magical properties. That's cool...Scully" ("He's Dead, She's Dead," 302). Ryan is sometimes on Castle's side, though to less of an extent, and Esposito is firmly rooted in the rational.

> **Castle**: Surrounded by skeptics.
> **Esposito**: It's called being a cop, bro. ("He's Dead, She's Dead," 302)

Castle, meanwhile, is determined to awaken Beckett's sense of mystery and wonder.

> **Castle**: Oh, let me guess. You don't believe in fate.
> **Beckett**: I was 3, and we didn't have a chimney. ("He's Dead, She's Dead," 302)
> . . .
> **Beckett**: Why is it so important to you that I believe all this stuff about fates and psychics and Santa Claus?
> **Castle**: Because if you don't believe in even the possibility of magic, you'll never ever find it. ("He's Dead, She's Dead," 302)

Their usual split prompts many fun moments in the series. Their books also provide a topic of contention:

> **Castle**: Wait, is that why you've been so upset? Because I let her *[Cosmo reporter]* read it before you?
> **Beckett**: I am the inspiration. I should be reading it before a reporter does.
> **Castle**: Why didn't you just say so?
> **Beckett**: Why didn't you just give it to me?
> **Castle**: Why didn't you ask?
> **Beckett**: Why didn't it occur to you?
> [Brief pause, and then he realizes she has a point]
> **Castle**: You'll have it by tomorrow.

Beckett: Good.
Castle: Good. ("Inventing the Girl," 203)

She finds herself searching for the "steamy" sex scene within.

Lanie: You tell me.
Beckett: What?
Lanie: Don't "what" me. Castle's lost love.
Beckett: Yeah. What about it?
Lanie: Girl, I'm gonna smack you. You work side by side every day. He writes a sex scene in his book about you that had me reaching for ice water. Now little miss bride shows up. Don't tell me you're not the least bit jealous.
Beckett: Oh, please. You've been inhaling too many autopsy fluids.
Lanie: Honey, just because *you* can't see what's goin' on doesn't mean anyone else doesn't see what's going on.
Beckett: Shut up.
Lanie: Mm-hmm. 'Cause I see it. You may not, but I do. ("A Rose for Everafter," 212)

The next hurdle comes when Beckett's mother's killer is discovered.

Beckett: It wasn't your fault, you know.
Castle: I overstepped. I came down here to say that I'm sorry... and that I'm through. I can't shadow you anymore. If it wasn't for me –
Beckett: If it wasn't for you, I would never have found my mom's killer. And someday soon I'm gonna find the sons of bitches who had him kill her. And I'd like you around when I do. And if you tell anyone what I'm about to say there's gonna be another shooting, but... I've gotten used to you pulling my pigtails. I have a hard job, Castle, and having you around makes it a little more fun.
Castle: ...Your secret's safe with me. ("Sucker Punch," 213)

Season two sees Beckett fall for Tom Demming, a robbery cop. During "Overkill" (221), Castle competes with Demming in crime-fighting. Martha mentions that sometimes he has to be able to know when he's been beaten, and Castle ends the episode seeing Demming and Beckett making out in the hallway. In "Food to Die For" (222), Beckett tells Castle (speaking about the love triangle in the case) that given the choice of a man she felt real passion for, but suspected would be unreliable, she would pick the safer man who wouldn't break her heart. Castle knows she's picking Denning over him.

As season two ends, Castle quits – allegedly for the summer, but as Ryan and Esposito point out, he doesn't seem to want to hang around watching her with her new boyfriend. After soul-searching, Beckett dumps her cop boyfriend, only to discover Castle is suddenly going to the Hamptons with Gina.

In season three he returns but doesn't call. When Beckett finds him at a crime scene with a gun, she arrests him for murder. She throws him off her case repeatedly, but he finally bets her he can solve it and she lets him win so she'll be forced to take him back.

> **Castle:** Do you know what these bodies are? A sign.
> **Beckett:** A sign?
> **Castle:** A sign. A sign from the universe telling us we need to solve this case together. You don't wanna let the universe down, do you?
> **Beckett:** You're not gonna go away no matter what I do, are you?
> **Castle:** I respect the universe.
> **Beckett:** Okay, fine. I will let you join me on this one case as long as you promise to do what I say, when I say it, and not to do any investigating on your own.
> **Castle:** I promise. You won't regret this.
> **Beckett:** I already do.
> **Castle:** Starting now. ("A Deadly Affair," 301)

On a case, a psychic tells Beckett "Alexander" will be important to her and save her life, and Castle reveals that's his real middle name ("He's Dead, She's Dead," 302).

Beckett dresses up stunningly in several episodes ("Home Is Where the Heart Stops," "When The Bough Breaks," "The Third Man," "The Final Nail," "The Limey," "The Lives of Others," "Hollander's Woods"). Each time, Castle is quite appreciative.

When 3XK fools Castle, Beckett comforts him and brings him coffee for the first time, empathizing with his pain ("3XK," 306). As season three goes on, once again, Beckett's mother's death resurfaces and brings them together:

> **Castle**: I don't hang around you just to annoy you, I don't ride off to murder scenes in the middle of the night just to satisfy some morbid curiosity. If that was all this was I would've quit a long time ago.
> **Beckett]**: Well, then, why do you keep coming back, *Rick*?
> **Castle**: *[Swallows]* Look, I may not have a badge – unless you count the chocolate one Alexis gave me for my birthday – but I'll tell you this: like it or not, I'm your plucky sidekick.
> **Beckett**: Plucky sidekick always gets killed.
> **Castle**: Partner, then.
> **Beckett**: Okay. ("Knockdown," 313)

Beckett starts dating Josh Davidson, a motorcycle rider who's also a cardiac surgeon. Though he saves her and Castle when they're locked in a freezer, the pair still have a sweet moment together, as she tells him "Thank you for being there" and he replies "Always" ("Countdown," 317).

Castle also feels jealousy about Beckett playing muse for another mystery writer:

> **Castle**: *[Drops his false humor]* Yes. Fine, it's true. I'm jealous. There, I said it. I-I want you all to myself, and to have you spending time with another writer? That upsets me! And if that makes me petty, so be it. Guilty as charged.
> **Beckett**: *[Smiles]* Actually, I kinda think it's sweet.
> **Castle**: You do?

> **Beckett**: I do. And that's why you don't have to worry about me hanging around with Conrad anymore. From now on I'm a "one writer" girl. ("The Dead Pool," 321)
>
> . . .
>
> **Castle**: Thank you.
> **Beckett**: Always. ("The Dead Pool," 321)

When they visit LA together, they share a hotel suite, and there are sparks between them:

> **Castle:** You know what I thought when I first met you?
> Beckett: Hm?
> **Castle:** That you were a mystery I was never going to solve. Even now, after spending all this time with you, I'm still amazed at the depth of your strength and your heart... and your hotness.
> **Beckett:** You're not so bad yourself, Castle. ("To Love and Die in L.A., 322)

To break the growing mood, she quickly leaves and shuts het door, but instead of going to bed she leans up against it. Castle is still sitting on the couch, his eyes trained on the door she just shut. However, by the time she goes back out, she's too late. Castle's door is shutting. Describing the near-kiss in LA, Andrew W. Marlowe explains, "Well, have you ever been in love with somebody who you're really good friends with? And you know it could all go bad?" (Mitovich, "In Review"). At season end, Castle confronts Beckett directly:

> **Castle:** No, you know what? I don't know what we are. We kiss, and then we never talk about it. We nearly die, frozen in each other's arms, but we never talk about it. So no, I've got no clue what we are. I know I don't want to see you throw your life away!
> **Beckett:** Yeah well last time I checked, it was my life, not your personal jungle gym. And for the past three years I've been running around with the school's funniest kid. And it's not enough.
> **Castle:** You know what? This isn't about your mother's case anymore. This is about you needing a place to

> hide. Because you've been chasing this thing so long
> you're afraid to find out who you are without it.
> **Beckett:** You don't know me, Castle. You think you do,
> but you don't.
> **Castle:** I know you crawled inside your mother's murder
> and didn't come out. I know you hide there, same way
> you hide in these nowhere relationships with men you
> don't love. You could be happy, Kate. You deserve to
> be happy. But you're afraid.. ("Knockout," 324)

As Beckett is shot and dying, Castle tells her, "I love you."
When she wakes, she tells him she doesn't remember
anything and asks for space.

They first sit on the swings together after Beckett
recovers from being shot (after three months without
calling) and she tells him she's no longer with Josh.

> **Castle:** So why did you guys break up?
> **Beckett:** I really, really liked him. But that wasn't
> enough. After my mother was killed, something inside
> me changed. It's like I built up this wall inside. And I
> don't know, I guess I just didn't want to hurt like that
> again. I know I'm not going to be the kind of person that
> I want to be, I know that I'm not going …
> **Beckett:** I'm not going to have the kind of relationship
> that I want until that wall comes down. And it's not going
> to happen until I put this thing to rest.
> **Castle:** Then I suppose we're just going to have to find
> these guys and take them down. ("Rise," 401)

Describing the beginning of season four, Andrew W.
Marlowe explains:

> There's subtext when she's saying, "I'm not going to
> have the relationship I want to have until I solve my
> mother's case." And now we're in a really interesting
> situation where he can't let her look into it, because
> she's going to be killed – that's really the impediment
> here. That allows us to continue with the Beckett-and-
> Castle tension and playfulness as we're moving
> forward. As you saw at the tail end, we had two very big
> revelations – that Castle was going to push forward on
> the [Johanna Beckett] case without her, and we get her

admission that she remembers. They both have these enormous secrets from each other this season that hopefully will color and play into the subtext of everything we're doing. If either of these secrets comes to light, the other party could see it as being a huge betrayal. (Mitovich, "In Review")

At episode end, she starts seeing psychologist Carter Burke and confides a great deal about her desire for Castle and the wall she keeps inside. She also tells him she has faked her amnesia. Similarly, Andrew W. Marlowe explains why Beckett lied to Castle about remembering:

Being the kind of person she is, I think she's not ready to deal with the emotional consequences of accepting what she heard. She has very strong feelings for Castle, which she recognizes but is concerned about acting on because she's concerned about what it will do to their relationship. She's also concerned that she's at a point where she's really fragile. She wants a real relationship, she doesn't want to be a "conquest," just another one of the many women he's been with. She feels like he's important in her life, and that she should be important in his – and she doesn't trust that yet. (Mitovich, "In Review")

However, Castle overhears Beckett talking to a suspect about trauma and realizes she's remembered all this time ("47 Seconds," 419). He begins shutting her out.

Kate: I'm telling you, something happened. Something changed. It's been weird between us lately.
Lanie: Lately? Kate, it's been weird for four years.
Kate: No, this is different. He's different. It's like he's pulling away.
Lanie: Well, can you blame him? He's probably tired of waiting.
Kate: Waiting for what?
Lanie: What do you think? The guy is crazy about you, and despite your little act, you're crazy about him. *(Kate looks at her.)* Oh, what, was that supposed to be some big secret?
Kate: Yes. No. Do you think he knows?

Lanie: You remember how he used to be? Girl on either arm. You really don't see that guy too much anymore. Why do you think that is? He's waiting for you.
Kate: Yeah, but Lanie...
Lanie: I know. You're dealing with stuff. But you cannot ask him to wait forever. Unless, of course, you're okay with him pulling away. ("The Limey," 420)

Kate: You think he remembers?
Castle: When a life altering moment occurs, people remember.
(After a pause.)
Kate: Well, maybe it's too big to deal with. Maybe he... can't face it just yet.
Castle: You think he ever will be?
Kate: Hopefully. If he feels safe. ("Undead Again," 422)

Castle: How does somebody put something like that behind them? He's gonna need therapy.
Kate: It helps. First he won't even be able to deal with it. It's gonna take everything that he's got to just put one foot in front of the other and get through the day.
Castle: I didn't know you were seeing a therapist.
Kate: Yeah, well, I didn't wanna make any excuses, I just wanted to put in the time, do the work. But I think I'm almost where I want to be now.
Castle: And where is that?
Kate: In a place where I can finally accept everything that happened that day. Everything.
Castle: I think I understand.
Kate: And, um, that wall that I was telling you about... I think it's coming down.
Castle: Well, I'd like to be there when it does.
Kate: Yeah, I'd like you to be there too.
Castle: Only, without the zombie makeup. ("Undead Again," 422)

At season end, he forces the issue and tells Beckett he's been protecting her all season.

Kate: How the hell could you this?
Castle: Because I love you. But you already know that, don't you? You've known for about a year.

Kate: Are you kidding me? You're actually bringing this up right now, after you told me that you just betrayed me?
Castle: Kate, listen to me –
Kate: Listen to you? Why should I listen to you? How am I even supposed to trust anything that you say
Castle: How are you s – Because of everything that we have been through together! Four years, I've been right here! Four years just waiting for you to just open your eyes and see that I am right here. And that I'm more than a partner. Every morning, I-I bring you a cup of coffee, just so I can see a smile on your face. Because I think you are the most remarkable... maddening... challenging... frustrating person I've ever met. And I love you Kate, and if that means anything to you, if you care about me at all, just don't do this. ("Always," 423)

He quits being her partner and goes home. Defiantly, she chases down the contract killer alone, and he nearly kills her. After this, she sits at their playground in the rain, staring at the other empty swing. Then she rushes to his apartment. She tells him, "He got away, and I didn't care. I almost died and all I could think about was you. I just want you," kisses him fiercely and pushes him into the bedroom ("Always," 423).

In season five they become a secret couple. "Everybody was worried about the *Moonlighting* curse," Fillion says. "But you can't look at it that way. Being a couple isn't the end of something – it's the beginning of something." (Sheffield). They have their squabbles as she's jealous of a sexy actress in the second episode, but they're mostly happy and unified. In "Still" (522), Beckett is stuck on a pressure-plate bomb, and Castle refuses to leave her, entertaining her through a clip show of flashbacks about their relationship.

However, as the season ends, both come to realize they've never defined their relationship. Kate considers a job working for the Feds in DC. To show his love for her, at their swingset, Castle proposes. "Whatever happens, and whatever you decide, Katherine Houghton Beckett will you marry me?" ("Watershed," 524).

As he adds after the season break, "Kate, I'm not proposing to you to keep you here, or because I'm afraid I'm going to lose you. I'm proposing because I can't imagine my life without you. If that means when things get difficult we have to figure them out then I'm willing to figure them out. Assuming you're willing to figure them out with me" ("Valkyrie," 601).

She goes off to DC but also accepts his proposal. The beginning of the sixth season has Castle and Beckett trying to manage their engagement while Beckett is working as a federal agent in DC. Of course, she's fired within a few episodes and they're back at the NYPD. The rest of season six is spent on wedding preparations – finding a date, venue, honeymoon, dress, song, and so on.

Castle is kidnapped on the way to their wedding and Beckett searches relentlessly for two months. He's finally found at sea, with amnesia, and together they work back to being comfortable with each other again. After Castle has an "It's a Wonderful Life" moment, seeing himself if he'd never met Beckett, they have a spontaneous wedding in "Time of our Lives" (706):

> **Beckett:** The moment that I met you, my life became extraordinary. You taught me to be my best self. To look forward to tomorrow's adventures. And when I was vulnerable, you were strong. I love you, Richard Castle. And I want to live my life in the warmth of your smile and the strength of your embrace. I promise you, I will love you. I will be your friend. And your partner in crime and in life. Always.
>
> **Castle:** The moment we met, my life became extraordinary. You taught me more about my life than I Knew there was to learn. You are the joy in my heart. You're the last person I want to see every night before I close my eyes. I love you, Katherine Beckett. And the mystery of you is the one I want to spend the rest of my life exploring. I promise to love you, to be your friend

and your partner in crime and life, 'til death do us part
and for the time of our lives.

After getting caught up in a mob scheme, Castle is
barred from working with the NYPD and becomes a
private investigator instead. In "Reckoning" (715), Tyson
kidnaps Beckett and Castle goes on a one-man hunt to
save her. After, he tells her, "I don't know how you did
it....Kept it together the two months I was missing. Two
days I didn't know where you were and it nearly killed
me." She thanks him for saving her and he replies,
"Always." As a reward for his heroism, Castle is allowed
back to work with the police.

At his Poe's Pen Career Achievement Award
ceremony at season end, Castle says, "Kate. Seven years
ago I thought I would never work again and then you
walked in the door and my whole world changed. You
were right, you said I had no idea. But now I do. This is
because of you, because of us. Always" ("Hollander's
Woods," 723). The dedication of *Driving Heat* is the last
line here. Indeed, most of the novels are dedicated to
Beckett, increasingly flowery as they're bonded together.

"The important thing to say about [Rick and Kate] is
that the show has always been and will always be about
their love affair," new showrunner Hawley says for season
eight. "But we're looking to add some drama to it, some
spark to it. We're going to have fun. It's going to be
emotional at times, it will be romantic.... It will be
everything." (Mitovich, "Castle Bosses").

The Character Arcs

Castle

Viewers may very well be responding to Castle, who began tailing NYPD homicide detective Kate Beckett (Stana Katic) for book research, because there's so much of Fillion in the fun-loving mystery writer. The quirks around Castle's edges – from the obsession with gadgets to the clever miming – are vintage Fillion, and while it's the actor who often rides a Xootr scooter to and from his trailer on set, that could just as easily be a trait of man-boy Richard Castle. The show's creator, Andrew W. Marlowe, a longtime Fillion fan from his days on *Buffy* and *Firefly*, thought as much when he cast him: "He's a guy who I thought had the many facets to show the many different kinds of faces of what it meant to be a man. To play the beleaguered son, the loving father, a potential love interest who's charming but someone who is also really annoying yet can get away with it – Nathan had that in spades." (Bierly et al.)

Castle was cast early as Nathan Fillion, the man who adores gadgets, fandom, and fun. His name may be an homage to Stephen King with another chess piece name, or it may pun on "Rich Asshole," as Rich Castle is a sound-alike. The character says of himself:

I was born during a howling thunderstorm on the first of April, shortly after midnight. According to the doctor, as I took my first breath the heavens shuddered with a thunderclap unlike any he had ever heard before... or since. Needless to say, after a birth like that, people expected great things. But I wasn't quite ready for the pressure, so I spent the next few years sucking my thumb and spitting up on people. (Richardcastle.net)

Richard Alexander Rodgers, who changed his name to Richard Edgar Castle, lives at 595 Broome Street, New York, NY 10013, with his mother and daughter. As the first episode shows, he was always something of a bad boy:

> **Beckett**: Mr. Castle, you've got quite a rap sheet for a bestselling author. Disorderly conduct, resisting arrest.
> **Castle**: Boys will be boys.
> **Beckett**: It says here that you stole a police horse?
> **Castle**: Borrowed.
> **Beckett**: Ah, and you were nude at the time.
> **Castle**: It was spring. ("Flowers for your Grave," 101)

He grew up with a single mother who could be neglectful as she pursued her acting career and left him with nannies. His father, of course, was a mystery. Castle adds:

> Given my birthdate, my mother called me her April Fools' baby, and every birthday she'd sit me down and solemnly tell me that I was adopted. The minute she had me going, she'd yell, "April Fools!" and we'd both laugh and laugh, and then she'd gently remind me that she had no idea who my father was. You'd expect this to bother me, but I kind of liked not knowing who he was. In my imagination he was something cool, like an astronaut, or a jungle explorer, or at the very least an insurance actuary assessing the risks of being an astronaut or jungle explorer. I suppose that making up stories about my father's identity was how I found my way to telling stories. I'd gotten a taste for it, and I liked it! (Richardcastle.net)

At age fourteen, Castle was sent to boarding school at Edgewyck Academy, where he was homesick and lonely until Damian Westlake befriended him. Damian was the editor of the literary magazine and he published a story of Castle's and told Castle that he had a real talent for writing. At the same school, Castle was in danger of flunking out, so he bought another student's paper. As he tells Beckett later:

> It changed how I saw myself. The teacher read the
> paper to the entire class as an example of great writing
> and I was applauded. It was the first time I was
> celebrated for anything and…it was a fraud. I – I was a
> fraud. That's when I learned how to write. I wrote and
> wrote, trying to be as great as everyone thought I was,
> trying to earn that applause. I'm still trying. ("The Wild
> Rover," 518)

Castle wrote most of his first book, *In a Hail of Bullets*,
at The Old Haunt, a bar he purchases during the series.
The book sold over three million copies. He wrote other
independent mysteries, then the celebrated Derrick Storm
series, which he ended by killing off his character in *Storm
Fall*, the book released in the first episode.

In the first episode, he also meets Detective Beckett.
A copycat killer is murdering people in the style of Castle's
books, and she calls him in to consult, making his wishes
come true.

> **Castle**: *[to his daughter Alexis]* I just want someone to
> come up to me and say something new.
> **Beckett**: Mr. Castle?
> **Castle**: [turning around holding a pen ready to give an
> autograph] Where would you like it?
> **Beckett**: *[holding badge]* Detective Kate Beckett,
> NYPD. We need to ask you a few questions about a
> murder that took place earlier tonight.
> **Alexis**: [taking the pen from him] That's new. ("Flowers
> for your Grave," 101)

After, he decides to write a book about Beckett,
reimagining her as NYPD homicide detective Nikki Heat
and himself as Pulitzer prize winning journalist Jameson
Rook. The pair have a steamy romance through the book
series, reflecting Castle's own sublimated feelings for
Beckett. Thanks to his friendship with the mayor, Castle
bargains for the chance to shadow Beckett for as long as
he wishes. Fillion notes that Castle has much to bring to

the partnership, though he's not a cop:

> I remember back in the day when we started *Castle*, he was a writer with a bunch of cops, cops who were trained to solve murders...And Castle didn't have that kind of training, and he had to bring something to the table. And what he brought to the table was 'I know a guy. I know this woman; she's connected to such and such. It was when I did research for this book.' He did all these books and all this research. He's no dummy, and he's made some amazing connections over the years and he would go and he would meet up with these guys and he'd have incredible things to learn from these people and they were connected and it was amazing. I would like to see more of that going on. (Highfill)

He sees crimes as stories, always attempting to look at motivations (even to the point of pulling out his comic book collection on one case). This technique, like his consultations with mystery writer friends, is surprisingly effective.

Castle has two ex-wives – the first is Meredith (Darby Stanchfield), Alexis's mother and a flighty actress, whom he describes as "Auntie Mame on meth" ("Always Buy Retail," 106).

> **Meredith**: We have had fun, haven't we?
> **Castle**: Oh, yeah.
> **Meredith**: Makes you wonder why we ever got divorced.
> **Castle**: I know, right? I mean, except for you having an affair with your director and moving to Malibu and serving me with divorce papers, I think we really had a chance. ("Always Buy Retail," 106)

He often sleeps with her when she coasts through town, but he considers her a terribly unhealthy relationship. He has custody of Alexis, and ruefully considers himself the more responsible parent of the pair of them. She visits a second time to cause havoc in "Significant Others" (510).

Castle meets up with his ex, Kyra Blaine, in "A Rose For Everafter" (212). Of course, she's getting married to someone else.

> **Castle**: We met in college. We were together nearly three years.
> **Beckett**: I didn't ask.
> **Castle**: Yes, you were not asking very loudly.
> **Beckett**: She's different from your ex-wives.
> **Castle**: What do you mean?
> **Beckett**: She's real. I didn't think you went for real. Tough break up?
> **Castle**: It was a long time ago. ("A Rose for Everafter," 212)

His second wife, Gina Griffon (Monet Mazur), is his publisher, and thus also still in his life. He spends the summer with her after season two, but they soon break it off as he's looking for real love. He also has many female fans that he dates on occasion:

> **Castle**: Life should be an adventure. Do you want to know why I killed Derrick? There were no more surprises. I knew exactly what was going to happen every moment of every scene. It's just like these parties they become so predictable, 'I'm your biggest fan, where do you get your ideas'.
> **Alexis**: And the ever-popular 'will you sign my chest.'
> **Castle**: That one I don't mind so much. ("Flowers for your Grave," 101)

"He's kind of a jerk," admits actor Nathan Fillion. "He's vain, he's immature. He lacks a certain amount of tact and consideration. I don't know how long I could hang out with that guy, without needing to kick him in the nuts a little bit" (Sheffield).

At the NYPD, he quits or is dismissed a few times, though each time he returns within a few episodes. Though he worries he's only playing cop, he's an excellent investigator and a better shot than Beckett, though he very rarely handles a gun in the field. Season seven sees him getting his Private Investigator license and an impressive office as he takes cases.

In "Target" (515), nice-guy Castle reveals he has a true edge as he tortures a man in interrogation to find out where his daughter has been taken:

> **Beckett:** Tell me what happened with Douglas Stevens.
> **Castle:** I appealed to his humanity.
> **Beckett:** I didn't think you had it in you.
> **Castle:** When it comes to saving someone I love, I do.

In "Hollander's Woods" (723), he shoots his assailant at point-blank range, indicating more lines he's finally willing to cross. The episode also reveals more of his backstory, as, as a child, he stumbles onto his first murder, a crime he's never able to solve until this episode.

Beckett

Billionaire Eric Vaughn notes in season five, "You graduated top of your class. You're the youngest woman in the history of the NYPD to make detective. You have the highest closure rate of anyone in the department and earlier this year you bucked every protocol to save a senator's life" ("The Squab and the Quail," 521). Detective Kate Beckett (Stana Katic) is twenty-nine in season one. Her home address is 2540 E. 3rd Street, New York, NY 10012, and her badge number is 41319. On meeting her, Castle reads a great deal upon looking at her:

> Well, you're not bridge and tunnel. No trace of the boroughs when you talk, so that means Manhattan, that means money. You went to college, probably a pretty good one. You had options. Yeah, you had lots of options, better options, more socially acceptable options, and you still chose this. That tells me something happened. Not to you. No, you're wounded, but you're not that wounded. No, it was somebody you cared about. It was someone you loved. And you probably could have lived with that, but the person

responsible was never caught. *[realizing he's overstepped]* And that, Detective Beckett, is why you're here.

At the time of her mother's murder, her father, a lawyer, succumbed to alcohol, but she helped him through it. Jim Beckett (Scott Paulin) remains a supportive, though somewhat distant figure in her life, showing up at Castle's door during season three and occasionally thereafter.

We learn that Beckett had a six-month relationship with Agent Sorenson, that ended with him leaving. ("Little Girl Lost," 109).

> **Beckett**: Six months.
> **Castle**: Six months what?
> **Beckett**: We dated for six months.
> **Castle**: I didn't ask.
> **Beckett**: Yeah, I know. You were not asking very loudly.
> **Castle**: I know, I'm like a Jedi like that.
> …
> **Castle**: Nice guy. I can see how it wouldn't work, though.
> **Beckett**: Really?
> **Castle**: Sure. Handsome, square-jawed, by the book.
> **Beckett**: And that's a bad thing?
> **Castle**: He's like the male you. Yin needs yang, not another yin. Yin yang is harmony. Yin yin is a name for a panda. ("Little Girl Lost," 109)

While Castle is the superfan of everything, Beckett reveals her own fannishness: for the scifi television show *Nebula 9*, for John Woo action films, for soap operas, for Frank Miller's comics. Her grandfather was a magician and she enjoys magic tricks as well. It's also revealed through the series that she was a teen model.

She puts up with Castle tagging along but soon discovers her cases are more fun with him around. Before him, she was incredibly serious about her work – her mother's murder goaded her to become a cop in the first place, and she is poignantly aware of the families and how they suffer through each case. Her mother's murder also comes to the forefront each season as she discovers small pieces of the puzzle. Of course, season three ends with Montgomery sacrificing himself for her, though he's unable to prevent her from getting shot.

After her return to life, she pretends she didn't hear Castle say he loved her and cuts off contact for months. Nonetheless, she begins seeing therapist Dr. Carter Burke (Michael Dorn) to try to reconcile both her shooting and Castle's declaration. Through the season, she suffers some PTSD and must rely on her friends:

> **Beckett:** *[Heading to the evidence room]* Espo, what are we doing back here?
> **Esposito:** I want to show you something. *[Pulls out a rifle]*
> **Beckett:** What is that?
> **Esposito:** The rifle that shot you.
> **Beckett:** You are way out of line.
> **Esposito:** Just look at it.
> **Beckett:** *[Backs away]* What the hell are you doing?
> **Esposito:** I've been where you are, I know what you're going through.
> **Beckett:** Javi, I'm fine.
> **Esposito:** You're not fine. You're just trying to act like you are. *[Holds up the rifle]* This is just a tool. It's a hunk of steel. It has no magical powers, and the person that fired it is not some all-powerful God. Just a guy with a gun. Just like the guy we've hunting now. And like every other bad guy, he's damaged goods.
> **Beckett:** [After a moment of silence] So am I.
> **Esposito:** That's right. And that's okay. You think it's a weakness? Make it a strength. It's a part of you. *[Hands the rifle out to her]* So use it. ("Kill Shot," 409)

Season four ends with her putting Castle before her mother's murder, though at the beginning of the following season, she discovers Senator Bracken is responsible. In season six, she finally finds her mother's hidden evidence and arrests him.

Beckett is an excellent detective, with an excellent

closure rate on her cases. Nonetheless, she finds herself yearning for something more ambitious. This arrives when she impresses the FBI at the end of season five. When Gates hears she went for an interview there, Gates tells her, "I just want to tell that…I gave you my highest recommendation….Kate, this is the kind of work you were meant to be doing. You'd be on the national stage utilizing all you talents. This is an incredible opportunity. I would have killed to have a shot at something like this when I was your age" ("Watershed," 524).

Beckett accepts the job, but finds she can't manage the moral compromise and is fired within a few months. She resumes her old job at the NYPD. When Castle vanishes before their wedding, she tracks him down with single-minded determination. After they marry in season seven, she moves out of her beloved apartment at last ("Last Action Hero," 709) and leaves it to her cousin.

She continues to have qualms about her lack of ambition:

> **Beckett:** Ensign Klemp has just been promoted to Captain. He's going to run the Nine Two….We started together, we graduated together, and he's going to be Captain and I'm just –
> **Castle:** The best homicide detective in the city?
> **Beckett:** No. I'm falling behind. ("Hong Kong Hustle," 717)

At last, she takes the captain's exam and passes, but is offered a different stunning opportunity,

> **Gibney:** Your future. We've been looking for someone like you. Someone who isn't corruptible. A certifiable hero who the people can get behind. Kate, you're bigger than what you're doing now. You know it. It's why you went to DC, why you took the captain's exam. You want a bigger stage and we want to give it to you. We think you have an amazing future.
> **Beckett:** Doing what?

> **Kaufman:** We'd like you to run for New York State Senate. ("Hollander's Woods," 723).

It's a tough decision, but she chooses captaincy at her beloved precinct....at least for now.

Alexis

Alexis Castle (Molly Quinn) is introduced as the serious teen doing homework at her rich father's party – a playmate for Castle but also often the adult of the relationship:

> **Castle**: When I was your age... I can't tell that story, it's wildly inappropriate, which oddly is my point. Don't you want to have wildly inappropriate stories that you can't tell your children?
> **Alexis**: I think you have enough of those for the both of us. ("Flowers for your Grave," 101)

She supports her father's work with the NYPD, though she's often frightened he'll be shot. For the most part, she plays the straight man to her father's and grandmother's obsessions, though their threesome is loving and supportive.

Of course, Alexis also has classic teen milestones:

> **Alexis:** Oh, my gosh, Dad! Dad, dad, dad!
> **Castle:** What is it?
> **Alexis:** Dad, he asked me! Dad, he asked me!
> **Castle:** Who asked you?
> **Alexis:** Owen. But I told him I had to ask you. But you'll say yes, right? 'Cause I told him yes. But you have to say yes, so say yes!
> **Castle:** Yes?
> **Alexis:** Yes!
> **Castle:** What am I saying yes to?
> **Alexis:** The junior-senior prom.

Wearing a stunning dress, she attends with Owen, a sweet fifteen-year-old. Though Castle's tempted to harass her date, he plays the loving, supportive, slightly worried father, and waits up for her as she gets her first kiss. Alexis assures him she'll always be his little girl ("A Death in the Family," 110).

She has several other infatuations, though to her irritation, her father checks up on her adorable music tutor.

> **Alexis**: No, no, quiet. Am I a trouble-maker, Dad? Do I get drunk, disobey authority, steal police horses...
> **Castle**: That –
> **Alexis**: naked? No. That'd be you. I seem to be the only person in this family blessed with good judgment, and yet, you don't trust me. ("Fool Me Once," 204)

At season two's end, she heads off for a summer program for high school students at a college, in coed dorms. She returns unscathed, though with a crush on a boy from the program.

Season three sees her falling in love, though her boyfriend Ashley (Ken Baumann) meets Castle when he brings home a gun from the case, making a strong impression on the young man. Ashley claims over and over in a panic that he respects them both and Castle decides, "I like him...he's respectful" ("Punked," 304). The relationship keeps growing as Alexis rat-sits Ashley's beloved pet Theodore ("Murder Most Fowl," 308). In the next episode, Castle meets his parents, who find him fascinating.

They try a long-distance relationship when Ashley goes off to Stanford on the other side of the country. Alexis tries skipping senior year and joining him, but is rejected from the university. They continue clinging to their relationship over the phone, but Alexis feels taken for granted and they finally break up in "Cops & Robbers" (407).

She interns with Lanie to Castle's disconcertment, as she's at his job, and working with the horrors of dead bodies. "Dr. Parish agreed to let me shadow her. I thought if I go to med school this would give me a better grasp of forensic pathology. I've learned so much in just two days," Alexis says eagerly ("Pandora," 415). Seeing her dressed more adult, he's shocked how grown up she seems. Alexis soon excels at her job:

> **Alexis:** Based on my reading of the coroner's report, I can see why Graham Morton's death was ruled natural causes. However-
> **Castle:** Ooh! There's a "however."
> **Lanie:** A very big "however." *[To Alexis]* Tell them.
> **Alexis:** There were some anomalies I found suspicious. Evidence of petechiae in both eyes. Fresh bruising on the right side of Mr. Morton's nose, which could have happened if, say, someone was holding a pillow over his face. *[Castle and Beckett look at each other and then back]* All in all, I think there is ample evidence that Mr. Morton was murdered.
> **Castle:** *[To Lanie]* Ample?
> [Lanie nods]
> **Castle:** *[Grinning]* Murdered. *[Grabs Alexis and hugs her]* I am just so proud.
> **Alexis:** Dad. Work. Boundaries.
> **Castle:** *[Letting her go]* Right. ("A Dance with Death," 418)

Though she's tempted by many universities, she finally chooses Columbia, though with the understanding that she will stay in the dorms and Castle will give her her space. In "Target" (515), however, she's kidnapped to Paris by a criminal conspiracy targeting her grandfather the spy. Castle saves her, but after, she's severely shaken.

In "Watershed," (524), Alexis goes to Costa Rica. She tells Castle, "I can't stop living my life because of what happened. And yeah, I still have nightmares. But that's one of the reasons I want to go. I don't want to let fear win."

She returns in season six with the fruitarian Pi (Myko Olivier), whom Castle dislikes. They stay at Castle's place, and then Alexis decides to move in with Pi to Castle's horror ("Time Will Tell," 605). Castle visits Alexis and Pi's new place and is appalled that it's cute and homey. He tells Beckett, "I was hoping for squalor. I was counting on squalor. Because Alexis cannot last in squalor. I was just hoping this whole thing would blow over. She would see Pi for the ambition free hippie that he is. And now he's morphed into some...new age crusader? It's a though he's turned being a charming man-child into a career" ("Get a Clue," 606). He and Alexis fight and she's angry for his judging her choices. However, Alexis's love finally fades for Pi and she asks to return home. Castle eagerly accepts.

> **Alexis**: All those things my dad said when I was moving out, about me making a mistake moving in with my boyfriend, he was right. I can see it so clearly now. Why didn't I then?
> **Beckett**: You were in the love haze.
> **Alexis**: The love haze?
> **Beckett**: It's like a drug. It makes intelligent people do... stupid things. And then it clears and you look around and you wonder "What was I thinking?" ("Room 147," 616)

She continues at Columbia, though she spends time with her family and vacations with them. Stranded on a plane in "In Plane Sight" (721), Alexis insists on doing the autopsy with Lanie's help and actually talks the villain into giving up the gun, offering empathy and honesty. Castle is desperately proud.

Season eight has her becoming Castle's PI associate, as she solves his cases while he's not around. Though he's reluctant to let her into his unsafe world, he is forced to accept that she's an adult.

Martha

Martha Rodgers (Susan Sullivan) is a stage actress on and off Broadway. She has been nominated for a Tony Award ("Home is Where the Heart Stops," 107). Through the show, she auditions for and acts in many roles, showing off many odd techniques – waking at 5am, saying only her first line for two days, obsessing over decade-old reviews. She's had a checkered career:

> **Martha**: Ugh, lord. I played an elf, Santa's Village. Uh, Lady Liberty. Lady Liberty outside some low rent tax service. And then – oh, no. The worst job. The worst job I ever had. I was terrible at it. They hated me. It just – I – I was – it was absolutely the – just completely.
> **Castle**: What was it?
> **Martha**: Secretary. ("Almost Famous," 307)

She also teaches acting classes in Castle's house sometimes. At one point, she becomes a life coach. Of course, she raised Castle all on her own, and helps to raise Alexis. She's a supportive mother and grandmother, if a bit self-absorbed.

In season two, an old flame from high school, Chet Palaburn, reconnects with her on social media.

> **Martha**: What will Chet think if he expects 1980s Martha, and present-day Martha shows up?
> **Castle**: You tell anyone I said this, and I'll deny it. And I'm only gonna say it once; 1980s Martha was pretty great, but present-day Martha is pretty spectacular, too. ("Kill the Messenger," 208)

They stay up all night talking and quickly fall in love once more ("The Fifth Bullet," 211). Castle jokingly asks, "It's been a few weeks. Do I need to sit him down and ask him his intentions?"

Martha retorts, "I am having way too much fun to worry about his intentions. Okay, he took me for lovely candlelight dinner, horse and carriage ride through Central Park where we watched the sun rise over the same boulder where we shared our first kiss."

In "Tick Tick Tick" (217), she moves in with him. At last he proposes, and Martha hesitates, needing a night to think it over. However, to her shock, Chet suddenly dies.

Later, she discovers he left her a million dollars, which she uses to open the Martha Rodgers School of Acting ("Lucky Stiff," 314). She continues to date on occasion, but has had no one truly serious since then.

Esposito

Javier Esposito (Jon Huertas) had a rough childhood. "My parents split up when I was five...Dad moved to Florida with his new wife. Most I ever got after that was a phone call and a postcard," he explains. ("Under the Influence," 512). He has a long juvenile record.

A Glock 17 is his primary weapon. Esposito's badge number is 41077. Before joining the NYPD, Esposito was U.S. Army Special Forces and served time in Iraq. As he tells Beckett, he suffered PTSD afterwards. On cases, he tends to be more macho, while Ryan is more compromising and more of a believer like Castle. He's a big fan of telenovelas, however.

Esposito also enjoys flirting with Lanie on the job:

> **Beckett**: How's it going up there?
> **Lanie**: I got tree branches poking my boobs and spotlights shining up my booty.
> **Esposito**: Could be worse. You could be wearing a skirt.
> **Lanie**: When I come down, I'm gonna smack you.
> **Esposito**: I'll be looking forward to that. ("Deep in Death," 201)

They're finally seen as a (secret) couple in "Poof You're Dead!" (312). However, Lanie and Esposito take a break after a double date where Jenny asks when they'll be getting married and they have a huge fight. ("Demons," 406). They work out their problems and continue to see each other – in "The Limey" (420), Lanie reveals that the two still enjoy the occasional "booty call" together.

In "Under Fire" (611), when Esposito is trapped in a burning building with Ryan, Lanie is terribly frightened.

They get back together while Castle is missing between seasons six and seven. However, Lanie finally throws a wrinkle into the relationship when she asks him to meet her parents and adds that she told them she and Javi are engaged ("Bad Santa," 710). He pretends for her, but after, he faces his feelings:

> **Esposito:** I have to say this. Lanie, being fake engaged to you made me realize how great we are together. But not the way that your parents are. (she exhales) Or Castle and Beckett, or Ryan and Jenny.
> **Lanie:** I know. I feel it too. I mean, I'm crazy about you –
> **Esposito:** Oh, I'm crazy about you, too. But just – you know, not…not in that way. And you deserve what they have.
> **Lanie:** We both do. ("Bad Santa," 710)

The episode "Den of Thieves" (221) has Esposito trying to avenge his old partner Ike, who died while trying to work the case against Mafia boss Victor Racine. Esposito is dismayed to discover his old partner is secretly alive and working to gain evidence against Racine. Esposito helps him exonerate himself after three years of struggle. He's also part of the conspiracy to hide Montgomery's role in the death of Beckett's mother from everyone, even Captain Gates.

"Under the Influence" (512) sees the detective befriend a troubled fourteen-year-old, insisting that he can relate. He finally insists on weekly call-ins so he can help the kid turn his life around. He also shares his own juvenile rap sheet.

> **Esposito:** Yeah. But it's all I knew. My dad was gone, my mom was working two jobs. In my neighborhood, you had to do what you had to do to survive. Not everybody made it.
> **Joey:** Is this where you tell me to man up and get my act together like you did?
> **Esposito:** No. It doesn't work like that. You need help. For me it was one of my teachers. Saw a future in me

that I didn't even see in myself. But it was up to me to
make a choice. To pick which road to go down. ("Under
the Influence," 512)

Ryan

Detective Kevin Ryan (Seamus Dever) was not in the
original sample pilot, but was added as the first episode
was padded out. Thus everyone called him "the new guy"
(*Flowers for your Grave* Commentary). Ryan's badge number
is 42344. A Glock 17 is his primary weapon, from when
he got his start in Narcotics. He keeps a blog called The
Ryan Report and believes in horror films.

In his early life, Ryan spent twelve years in Catholic
school. He grew up in the Bronx with two older sisters —
one of whom now has a nephew who loves *Captain
Underpants*. This may be Gwen, seen in season seven.

Esposito is his best friend, though Ryan is much more
of a believer, even spinning wild theories when Castle isn't
around. Their bromance is central to the story.

> **Ryan**: Some guy are just hopeless. (picks up phone)
> Hey, Honey. Yeah, I was just thinking about you,
> thought I'd call you. Well, just wanted to call to say I
> miss you. Yeah.
> **Esposito**: Some guys are just pathetic.
> **Ryan**: I don't know. About 7:00.
> **Castle**: Don't be jealous. He still loves you. ("Suicide
> Squeeze," 215)

In "Kick the Ballistics" (404), he falls into a panic
when he discovers that his old service weapon, taken by
Jerry Tyson has been used in another killing.

His romance with Jenny Duffy-O'Malley proceeds
slowly and largely offscreen: Ryan is celebrating his two
week anniversary with his "girlfriend" in "Little Girl Lost"
(109). His friends believe she's fictional, however, until
she appears in "The Mistress Always Spanks Twice" (216).
Ryan asks Jenny's parents for permission to marry her,

then, though he had planned a helicopter ride at Castle's advice, he simply kneels and asks her in the precinct, surrounded by all their friends ("Nikki Heat," 311). Ryan and Jenny get married in "Till Death Do Us Part" (411). She's played by Seamus Dever's real life wife, Juliana Dever.

In season five, Ryan and Jenny struggle to get pregnant. The Ryan-centric episode "The Wild Rover" (518) reveals how he was once an undercover agent taking down the Irish mob. He goes back in, nearly dying. "Why would he do a thing like this? Maybe he thinks he has something to prove. You know, because of all our...pregnancy stuff," Jenny worries. At episode end, however, Jenny reveals that they're pregnant.

He and Esposito are trapped in a burning building and nearly killed in "Under Fire" (611). Dying, he calls Jenny, who's gone into labor, and asks her to name the baby after Esposito if he's a boy or for her grandmother if she's a girl. The team rescues the pair and he escapes the building only to find Jenny has given birth in a waiting ambulance. She tells him, "Kevin, I'd like you to meet...Sarah Grace."

Covered in body glitter and alcohol, Ryan reveals he's busy after hours: "Do you realize how much it's going to cost to send Sarah Grace to college? A quarter of a million dollars. That's for a state school. I – got a second job working nights." He reluctantly reveals it's being the bouncer at the male strippers' club Men-hattan. Esposito gets him a Security speedo as a joke ("Clear & Present Danger," 703).

"At Close Range" (718) sees him taking a security guard job with his brother-in-law, Frank Kelly. However, he's forced to arrest Frank, when he discovers the man is an accessory to murder, as he's been taking payoffs to slip people in backstage at a concert or give passes to fringe journalists.

Frank: I messed everything up. Even with a plea deal I'm going to jail.
Ryan: No, you don't know that.
Frank: Gwen's going to hate me. For lying. And for not being the man I said I was.
Ryan: She's strong, Frank. Stronger than you think. ("At Close Range," 718)

Montgomery

Captain Roy Montgomery (Ruben Santiago-Hudson) genuinely loves his wife and two daughters. He's a bit superstitious, as he reveals in the mummy episode, and is dedicated to the job – he vows to retire every few years but never quite pulls it off. Like Ryan and Esposito, he appears to like Castle, but tales Beckett's side in police and personal matters for the most part. He reveals that he was not coerced into allowing Castle to tail Beckett, but chose to accept it:

Montgomery: You want Castle gone? He's gone.
Beckett: I...what...what about the mayor?
Montgomery: This is my house, Kate. The mayor doesn't call the shots here. I do. You ought to know that by now.
Beckett: But I...I...
Montgomery: I could have kicked Castle to the curb years ago, any time I wanted to. Only reason I kept him around this long is because I saw how good he was for you. Kate, you're the best I've ever trained. Maybe the best I've ever seen. But you weren't having any fun before he came along. We speak for the dead. That's the job. We are all they've got once the wicked rob them of their voices. We owe them that. But we don't owe them our lives.
Beckett: He said that we can't win this.
Montgomery: He's right. I've spent most of my life walking behind this badge and I can tell you this for a fact. There are no victories. There's only the battle. And the best that you can hope for is that you find someplace where you can make your stand. If this is your spot? I will stand with you. ("Knockout," 324)

On meeting Beckett, he knows she can be an amazing homicide cop and makes her his personal project. He also feels he owes her a career, as he was involved in her mother's murder.

When young, he was involved in a scheme to hold mobsters and criminals for ransom, with the money going to someone who eventually became senator. However, he recorded their conversation, giving it to Johanna Beckett just before her death. In the third season finale, he's ordered to trap Beckett and leave her to be shot or his own family will die. He chooses to sacrifice himself instead, leaving an insurance policy in place to protect his protégé.

> **Beckett**: Give me a name. You owe me that, Roy.
> **Montgomery**: No, Kate. I give you a name, I know you. You'll run straight at him. I might as well shoot you where you stand.
> **Beckett**: That's why you brought me here, isn't it? To kill me?
> **Montgomery**: No, I brought you here to lure them.
> **Beckett**: You baited them?
> **Montgomery**: And now they're coming. I need you to leave. They're coming to kill you and I'm not going to let them. I'm going to end this. ("Knockout," 324)

Gates

Victoria Gates (Penny Johnson Jerald) joins in season four as the new captain. She's nicknamed "Iron Gates" and started her career as a detective in Internal Affairs. In fact, Beckett is the youngest woman in the NYPD to make detective, six weeks younger than Gates. While she appears to admire Beckett, she barely tolerates Castle most of the time, always coldly calling him "Mr. Castle." On one occasion, she begins to like him after he gives her a china doll to complete her set, but when he smashes them both, seeking clues, she turns frosty again.

A few of her family members appear as Gates mentions a loving husband. Her mother-in-law irritates her, however. Elizabeth Weston, the US Attorney for the southern district arrives in "The Greater Good" (619). She's Gates's sister.

> **Gates:** There's a history.
> **Beckett:** Mmm.
> **Gates:**1998. I had just been made head of Internal Affairs. Elizabeth was in the DA's office. We called ourselves the dynamic duo. At the time Elizabeth was closing in on a heroin ring in east New York and they had an undercover inside. His testimony was key to the case, but ...
> **Beckett:** He was dirty?
> **Gates:** He skimmed a few eight balls off the very boss Elizabeth was building her case around. When my office caught him reselling it, she came to me. Begged me not to file charges. Asked me to think of the greater good. (she pauses) I did my job that day, too. It hasn't been the same between us since.

Gates suspects that once again her sister is valuing expediency over the rules. "Do you think I'm blind? Bringing down someone as big as Burman, you'd be able to write your own ticket. The mayor's office, attorney general. Everything you always dreamed of," she says. Despite their history, they manage to compromise and work together on the case.

At the beginning of season eight, it's revealed that she was promoted to the new deputy chief, leaving Beckett to become precinct captain. In a message posted via Twitter, Jerald said, "To my Castle fans around the world, as of late yesterday I am surprised and saddened to learn that I will no longer be a part of the Castle family. Thank you all for your support and love. Hugs from PJJ" (Mitovich, "Penny").

Lanie

> **Lanie:** Getting a drink with me after work instead of getting your freak on with writer boy?
> **Beckett:** What? He is annoying, self-centered, egotistical, and completely-

Lanie: Fun. And take it from me, girlfriend, you need some fun. I mean, how bad can he be?
Beckett: [answers phone] Beckett.
Castle: [excitedly] Guess who's got a date with a prostitute! ("Hell Hath no Fury," 104)

Lanie Parish (Tamala Jones) acts as Beckett's gal pal in most scenes, urging her to get together with Castle. She has little plot arc beyond this, save in her romance with Esposito, though her parents visit in "Bad Santa," (710). She's seen dressing up stunningly in "The Double-Down," "Reality Star Struck," "The Blue Butterfly," "That 70s Show," and many other episodes. While delivering her autopsy reports and supporting Beckett in her love life, she nonetheless offers lots of fun and personality.

Nikki Heat Books

\	*Heat Wave*	(2009)
\	*Naked Heat*	(2010)
\	*Heat Rises*	(2011)
\	*Frozen Heat*	(2012)
\	*Deadly Heat*	(2013)
\	*Raging Heat*	(2014)
\	*Driving Heat*	(2015)

In a fun moment of fiction becoming reality, the Nikki Heat books went from show conceit to real books in stores. They even became *New York Times* Bestsellers. Each season, Castle gets in a quick mention or two of book tours and commercials for his latest release.

In tone, the books are violent and provocative from the first moments:

> The violent splash of ice and blood had already baked into the sidewalk in the minutes since the fall. As Heat stepped over there, she noted that the cafe umbrellas and the stone walls of the building also wore dried blood, ice spatter, and bits of tissue. She got as close to the wreckage as she dared without contaminating the scene and looked straight up. (*Heat Wave* 2)

The novels also certainly have their salacious side – in *Heat Wave,* Nikki Heat, coming out of the bathtub then air drying by walking around naked in her apartment, is attacked by a brute who plans to rape and murder her. She defeats him, but this involves a drawn out fight (still naked) and then chasing him up her fire escape while…less than dressed.

Nikki Heat

Beckett: She's naked on the cover again, isn't she?
Castle: Kinda yeah...
Beckett: That's great. No one's gonna make fun of me... ("A Deadly Game," 224)

Nikki Heat is a tough cookie from her first line of the novels. A young cop is checking her out, and she tells him, "Make you a deal. I'll watch my ass, you watch the crowd" (*Heat Wave* 2). By contrast, Rook shows up quipping, "It's raining men."

While her mother's murder defines her, the details are changed (unsurprisingly for Castle's character in a moment of sensitivity). Nikki Heat was nineteen, with her parents a year divorced. While in the store getting cinnamon sticks for the Thanksgiving pies, she called her mother and actually heard the murder take place in their apartment. "Had she really siphoned off all her rage, or merely clamped a lid on it?" the book wonders (*Heat Wave* 8). She turned from an English major interested in theater to a cop.

This background defines the driven, sensitive cop as she tells the grieving wife, "Murders are not numbers to me. A person died. A loved one. Someone you thought you were eating dinner with tonight is gone. A little boy has lost his father. Someone is responsible. And you have my promise I will see your case through" (*Heat Wave* 8). All this mirrors Beckett on the show:

Joanne: No, don't press conference me, Detective. Alright? I work in public relations. So you can save your speech, because I have heard them all. Alright? I'm the one who drafts all of that pathos after airline crashes and E. coli poisonings. "Our... Our hearts go out to the victims' families." Our hearts? I mean, what does that even mean? She said she felt like baking. She wanted me to come over, but I was busy. I was busy. And now she's dead.

> **Beckett:** Joanne. Listen to me. You're going to want to play out every possible scenario in the next couple of days. If only you'd been there. If only you'd come by. If only you didn't work late. And I'm telling you, it's not your fault. The ones to blame are the monsters that murdered your mom. This isn't a speech. It's not a platitude. It's a promise. I am going to do everything in my power to make sure that they pay for what they did. ("Home is Where the Heart Stops," 107)

Of course, she's tough, a martial artist who dominates the interrogation room and can control any situation:

> Nikki Heat had been in all sorts of interrogations and interviews with every stripe of lowlife in God's creation and those too damaged to make the-list. The wiseguys and the crazies thought because she was a woman they could rattle her with some leering porn-movie trash talk. A serial killer once asked her to ride in the van so he could pleasure himself on the way to the penitentiary. Her armor was strong. Nikki had the investigator's greatest gift, distance. Or maybe it was disconnection. (*Heat Wave* 59)

Rook writes about his first ride-along with Nikki for *First Press,* and makes her instantly famous, while others in her department are hurt at being left out. Once again, she's the muse for his writing, though she's the one to face much of this fallout.

Jameson Rook

Rook has written entertainment pieces about Bill Clinton, Mick Jagger, and Bono, but also risked his life doing cutting edge journalism in Darfur and Chechnya (where he was taken hostage). He's nearly killed spying on the West African coast and done work to aid Appalachian coal miners. All this has earned him two Pulitzers. He adds that the series of articles he wrote about his month underground with the Chechen rebels are being optioned for a movie (*Heat Wave* 8-9). Basically, he's a more exciting version of Castle, racing around the world doing real hard-hitting journalism.

His personality is much like Castle's as he quotes pop culture and flirts with Nikki, offering her gentleness and sensitivity while always having her back. His middle name is Alexander, like Castle's. Rook also writes romance novels as Victoria St. Clair. In his aptly named *Castle of her Endless Longing,* a man, "handsome in a roguish way" offers "Lady Kate Sackett" a "ride along" (*Heat Rises* 301).

While Nikki Heat is a powerful fighter, Rook hurls a plastic plate and salad bar ice at a fleeing suspect, attempting to take her down with Frisbee skills (*Deadly Heat* 168). He can take care of himself, but is more loveable goofball than cop.

Nikki/Rook Romance

In the books, Rook sends Nikki an art print of *Carnation, Lily, Lily Rose* just to make her smile (*Heat Wave* 79). As with Castle, he flirts and teases.

After Heat is attacked in her apartment, Rook insists on tailing her home, where, surprised, she kicks him in the jaw. She invites him up to put ice on it and lights candles as the electricity is out. "She felt a naughty thrill and smiled about how blackouts and hot nights brought on a certain lawlessness. Maybe she did need guarding – from herself" (*Heat Wave* 100). They start revealing personal truths and break out the tequila, then Nikki leads him to the bedroom. There's more than a trace of Castle's wish fulfillment in the writing. She also uses the line "you have no idea," said between them at the beginning of the show and in their wedding vows.

In the morning, she pushes him away, insisting on keeping things professional on the job. However, when the case is finally solved, as Rook asks, "Is the solution for me to give up our working relationship?" she drags him upstairs as she insists she has energy to burn (195). The heat wave breaks and they kiss in the rain.

By the second book, they've broken up. However, she

comes close to fainting when she discovers Rook is in trouble (*Naked Heat* 112). After he has a brush with death, leaving her filled with "post-trauma fragility" after fearing he was dead, she invites him over and they spend a steamy night dining on the rooftop then getting romantic, with plenty of metaphors about Nikki's "heat" (116).

In book three, he's on assignment far away, but Nikki is hurt when he returns without calling and appears in the celebrity pages having a glitzy dinner with his agent. Of course, they soon settle their differences. This book ends like the third season – only this time Rook is the one shot while Heat pleads with him to live.

At the end of *Frozen Heat*, he proposes and in *Driving Heat*, she accepts. Presumably, they're well on their way to becoming Castle and Beckett.

Captain Montrose

He has little personality in books one and two. Book three, he is clearly Captain Montgomery, though in the books he was recently widowed (presumably so Castle can leave the real grieving widow out of his story and give her some privacy). He's described as tall, Black and bald, with a kind face and a birthmark on his cheek (*Heat Rises* 19). Unlike Montgomery, Charles Montrose was never on the take, but is killed in book three for trying to unravel the vast conspiracy within the precinct.

Captain Irons

Captain Montrose is killed in book three while fighting corruption, and the pencil-pusher Captain Irons takes over (in a nod to at least the name of Captain "Iron" Gates). Irons is not Gates in personality, but a lazy desk jokey who cares only about public relations. He is a dull, fat, by-the-book pencil pusher who fixates on a simpler street death and dismisses Montrose's as suicide.

The department offers her Irons' job, but Nikki Heat prefers to go out and catch criminals than work behind a desk. Their relationship goes on to become mildly adversarial. As Heat thinks: "From her perspective, he was an organizational survivor concerned more with career than justice, someone she constantly had to outthink or outmaneuver to get the job done right" (*Frozen Heat* 15).

He also begins sleeping with the squad's most inept detective: "Nikki had learned the hard way that the best way to contain the damage Sharon Hinesburg caused on a case was to give her assignments where her laziness and sloppy detail work would do the least harm" (*Frozen Heat* 20). Corruption runs rampant while he's in charge.

Raley and Ochoa

Sean Raley and Miguel Ochoa are often identified by the joint nickname "Roach." Raley's nickname around the department is Sweet Tea – on the show, Ryan's nickname is actually Honey Milk, a drink he prepares for Jenny that the others got wind of. When Nikki is suspended in the third book they quietly help her. Lauren the mortician and Ochoa appear to be an item. They're clear stand-ins for Ryan and Esposito, with little changed about their characters.

Other Characters

Margaret Rook is Jameson Rook's mother, and Lauren Parry, the M.E. Both have identical personalities to their show counterparts, as does Heat's therapist Ron King, though there's no trace of Alexis.

Nikki Heat's father is still an alcoholic, while Beckett's is a recovering one. Nikki's father is also resistant to investigating his wife's murder again. Nikki's mother, Cynthia Trope Heat, was a talented concert pianist, though she gave up the life to teach...and pursue her own secret agenda.

Tomasso "Fat Tommy" Nicolosi runs enforcement for the mob and consults with Rook on occasion. Meanwhile, Jeanne Callow, Rook's agent, appears interested in him.

Rounding out the detective squad are *Firefly* shoutouts Malcolm and Reynolds. Rook says, in a blatant homage, "I can't put my finger on it, but there's something I like about Malcolm and Reynolds" (*Frozen Heat* 123). In addition, Randy Feller is young and often makes crude "class clown" jokes about the murders. He's also hot for Nikki. Rook finds his name suspiciously like an advertisement for his behavior.

Esposito complains on the show, "Derrick Storm? Nikki Heat? Jameson Rook? Would it kill you to name someone Gonzalez every once in a while?" ("Watershed," 524). Castle seems to take his advice with the brilliantly competent detective from the Hamptons, Detective Sergeant Inez Aguinaldo (who flips on the less-helpful one of "Murder, He Wrote").

Plots

Book one begins with a millionaire falling from his apartment. It's finally revealed that he was pushed. Partners Heat and Rook unravel his life into a series of lies – he had affairs, his wife had affairs, they were nearly broke. His dazzling art collection isn't what it seems and neither is his nanny. More important to the story are the brute who tries to assault Nikki Heat, and her relationship with Rook, which she finally consummates.

Naked Heat features the death of a much-hated gossip columnist. In what appear homages to the show, suspects and witnesses include a pop star, celebrity chef, Rook's mother, pro baseball player, a 22-year-old hooker who's actually the columnist's illegitimate daughter, talk show host, politician into S and M, Fat Tommy the Mobster, a dog walker/Julliard actor, and a hotel concierge. Petar, Nikki's old boyfriend, shows up. The gossip columnist actually revealed the truth in a book everyone's desperate to get their hands on, possibly a nod to Castle himself and his true-life fiction.

Heat Rises begins with a priest's death at an S and M club. However, Heat soon discovers that the priest was hiding a videotape wanted by a vast conspiracy...and her captain knows all about it. When he dies in an apparent suicide, then she is suspended, she discovers her partnership with Rook is her only chance to crack the case. They discover a network of cover-ups within the police and track down the secret Montrose was killed to protect.

In *Frozen Heat* a woman is frozen and stuffed in a suitcase. This parallels several show cases, complicated by the fact that Nikki Heat recognizes the suitcase – it's her own, stolen by her mother's killer. There's also a treasure hunter, an insurance investigator, a young biochemist who now competes in dog shows, and the sex goddesses phone line, all nods to *Castle* episodes. Rook guides her to stop working the present day case (which Irons throws her off of in his pedantic, corrupt way) and explore her mother's past. A startling picture emerges of the piano teacher who's secretly a spy. In the end, Nikki discovers the murderer is someone she trusted utterly, and she's devastated. She begins counseling and confesses that Rook is the only one she really trusts now. On the final page, she plays her mother's piano for the first time since the murder, and discovers a code in the sheet music.

Deadly Heat continues her attempt to unravel her mother's murder with the same criminals on the loose. There's a conspiracy to release a smallpox virus in New York, which Nikki most stop. As she teams up with Homeland Security – including Rook's old girlfriend there – she discovers moles passing on information, both there and within her own police department. In all this chaos, Rook is the only one she can trust. The book begins with health inspector Roy Conklin's body in a pizza oven, then a dead anchor from WHNY (From "Cloudy with a Chance of Murder," 502). There's also talk of making a *Nikki Heat* movie, and the comment comes up that

"Nathan [Fillion] would be perfect for casting, if he's available" (*Deadly Heat* 156)

Illegal immigrant Fabian Beauvais (who nods to the immigrants of "Always Buy Retail") falls from the sky in *Raging Heat*. Soon after, more murder victims are found, tortured. Worse yet, Beckett discovers Beauvais was fixing houses in the Hamptons, next door to Commissioner Keith Gilbert, "billionaire, power broker, senatorial hopeful, and golf buddy with the mayor" (*Raging Heat* 283). He soon becomes her chief suspect, but the higher-ups keep ordering her to drop the case, since all her evidence is circumstantial. This makes her fight harder to convict him, with a terrible hurricane coming and her promotion to an international task force on the line. Meanwhile, Rook fears she's being less than objective, and they're thrown into work-related conflict. Of course, everything comes together in an apocalyptic finish.

Salena Kaye is a villain in *Frozen Heat* and *Deadly Heat*, whose name mirrors Catwoman's and the ex-art thief on the show. In the Hamptons they call on an unnamed bestselling mystery writer who insists he's "Got Connelly, Nesbo, and Lehane waiting for me and Nick & Toni's, but that's all right. Good for humility" (*Raging Heat* 56). One assumes this is Castle.

Driving Heat begins with Heat as she starts her first day as captain of the precinct. The murder victim, however, is Heat's counselor, Ron King. This happens just as her engagement to Rook is filling her with anxiety. The pair are thrown into opposition as Rook refuses to share what he knows about the case because of his journalistic investigation. Heat actually threatens to imprison him before he reveals he's investigating a criminal conspiracy to cover up a faulty car part. This is being released by Forenetics, run by multi-billionaire Tangier Swift. However, it appears he's really the fall guy for a far different conspiracy as a lone man checks off a list of his enemies...and Rook and Heat are on that list!

Castle's Stand-Alone Mysteries

Richard Castle's first novel, *In a Hail of Bullets,* was written during his college years in a bathroom stall at The Old Haunt. This novel won the Nom-DePlume Society's Tom-Straw-Award for Mystery Literature. He has many independent mysteries that followed, though today they are all "out of print" as the Castle website explains (though synopses are available). Of course, he mentions them occasionally on the show.

In a Hail of Bullets stars rookie NYPD detective David McAllister – perhaps this is how Beckett got into the series. McAllister finds a murdered Broadway actress, and digs deeper when the main suspect suddenly commits suicide. In a fascinating parallel to the political episodes of *Castle,* McAllister finds the most powerful people in the city have a stake in this case. One hopes the actress plot wasn't a shot at Castle's mother.

Death of a Prom Queen stars valedictorian Cassie Evans in Saltee, North Carolina. With her classmates being killed off, Cassie must find the killer in time. Psychologist Norma Kent stars in *One Bullet, One Heart.* She suspects her patient, alpha male Jason Reese, is the town's new serial killer, shooting lovely young women. But as she begins investigating him, he does the same to her. *Flowers for Your Grave* has journalist Leroy Fine unraveling the case of the serial killer "The Florist" to regain everything he has lost. Rookie detective Alexandra Jones of *Kissed and Killed* is investigating deaths and dismemberments among the wealthy. Her leads take her to the fashion industry where those no longer beautiful are tossed aside. Of course, once there, she becomes a target as well. Most of the detectives are ordinary people, much like Castle himself. One is even a writer.

Some of the stories are more thriller than cozy mystery: In *A Skull at Springtime*, student Rachel Lyons is planting trees in remote Washington. When she discovers a field of corpses, she must escape back to civilization before she is the next to die. *Hell Hath No Fury* has Professor Adam Parel move to Jessup, Oregon to finish his first novel. He discovers a sinister side to the town as people have gone missing here for decades, thanks to an obsessive cult that will stop at nothing, including killing strangers like himself. *When it Comes to Slaughter* stars police officers Chief Derrick Olson and Deputy Ana Ruiz solving the sudden, brutal murders of two families in their sleepy town of Fair Haven Vermont. Rumors of a scarecrow-like creature with hatchets for hands prowling the countryside and deadly secrets make this a sensational and chilling tale.

At Dusk We Die tells of Ben Meltzer, who must flee town with his family when attacked by Satan's Creed, a gang of biker-vampires. *A Rose for Everafter* begins at the Blessed Sacrament School for Girls, where Sister Mary Grace investigates the murders of the girls there, whose bodies are turning up in shallow graves, wrapped in shrouds of white and grasping a red rose in their cold dead hands. With these violent, sensational stories of monsters and gothic violence, it's clear why Castle is always the one to offer outlandish theories and belief in the occult — they're what inspired these books.

Derrick Storm Books

Fictional Novels

- *Deadly Storm*
- *Gathering Storm*
- *Storm's Last Stand*
- *Storm Rising*
- *Unholy Storm*
- *Storm Season*
- *A Calm Before Storm*
- *Storm Warning*
- *Storm's Break*
- *Storm Approaching*
- *Driving Storm*
- *Storm Fall*

These are casually labeled "out of print" on Castle's website. Indeed, there is a full website, loaded with synopses and background on the author. "The deeper and richer you can make the audience experience for the show," Marlowe says, "the more loyal your audience is going to be" (Truitt).

In the first of the Derrick Storm series, *Deadly Storm*, Private Investigator Derrick Storm is recruited by the CIA's Clara Strike. In *Gathering Storm*, he is asked to protect the Swiss Ambassador's daughter from a KGB agent. *Storm's Last Stand* sees Derrick dredge up his past to solve an old friend's death. In *Storm Season*, Derrick bugs the hotel suite of an African head of state, but throws himself deeper into the investigation when he hears a woman's terrifying scream over the wire. *Storm Rising* has Derrick team up with a jewel thief to catch another, in

Paris. He seeks the murderer of his friend, Attorney Sam Strummel, in *Storm Warning*. *Storm's Break* has him stopping a Panama kingpin from human trafficking runaway teenage girls. In *Storm Fall*, Derrick's life is being sabotaged, and his investigation ends in his death.

Bad girl Clara Strike, a ruthless CIA operative and the love of Storm's life is a main character. "There's a similar Castle/Beckett dynamic in Storm and Strike," Castle creator Andrew Marlowe says, plus plenty of Castle's self-deprecation. "It captured both the spirit of who Castle is on the show and the spirit of his prose in the Nikki Heat novels" (Truitt).

The first episode of the show begins with Castle's book party for *Storm Fall*, in which he kills off his bestselling character, to the dismay of his publisher ex-wife and many others. "A Death in the Family" (110) reveals one of Castle's many 'sources' of information as Sal Tenor, the mobster, who gave Castle information about how the mob works for *Storm Warning*. He casually mentions other books, including *Tropical Storm*, which he never finished. "I started the book. I threw it out. It was…supervillain controls the weather…it was – it was terrible" ("Driven," 701).

Deadly Storm is adapted into comic book form and shows up in "Heroes & Villains" (402) at the same time as in real life. This subplot continued, with three other real-world graphic novels "adapting" Castle's old Derrick Storm novels. Thereafter, real book announcements for all the novels and comics appear at least once per season through Castle's book tours and media appearances. "Having books and graphic novels was always in Marlowe's mind when pitching the show. He put all that on the back burner as he tried to get it on the air, but when Castle began to gain a strong following, Marlowe decided to revisit those ideas" (Truitt).

Derrick Storm

Jones of the CIA thinks, "There was one man in his contact list whose training, intelligence, and tenaciousness were a match for this particular killer. He reached for his phone and called Derrick Storm" (*Storm Front* 13). Derrick Storm once killed an enemy agent with an ice cream scoop. He's ambidextrous. In a car chase, he makes weapons out of everything loose in the car, MacGyver style (*Storm Front* 257). He loves all the CIA gadgets and is an expert mountaineer (*Wild Storm* 122). Of his many weapons, Storm calls his beloved .44 Magnum Dirty Harry. He's skilled in car chases, though he prefers a Ford to flashier vehicles, and keeps them stashed all over the US.

> There had been a time in his life – before he'd met Jones – when Storm had been just another down-on-his-luck private detective with too many bills and not enough clients. He'd spent his days and nights peeping through windows at no-tell motels photographing cheating spouses and spying on able-bodied men who'd filed false workman's compensation claims citing "bad backs." Storm had scraped by. Barely.
>
> But then Clara Strike had entered his world and turned it upside down. The CIA field officer had enlisted Storm's help in a covert operation being run on American soil. Technically, the CIA was forbidden to operate inside the U.S., so she'd needed Storm as a front man. She'd taken advantage of his expert tracking skills, his patriotic spirit, and his then-trusting nature. She'd introduced him to Jones, and it had been Jones who'd drawn him further and further into the CIA's web. (*A Raging Storm*, ch. 4)

These events appear in *Deadly Storm*. He's a hero, with uncompromised morality unlike many in the CIA. His humble start and code of ethics appear responsible. When asked why he saves the world, he explains that morality isn't relative:

> "I believe there is such a thing as absolute bad and absolute good. And yes, there is a full spectrum of shades in between, which is where most people live. But when I see things that are a lot closer to the bad end of the spectrum, and see that people who are a lot closer to the good end of the spectrum are going to be hurt, I feel I have to act." (*Wild Storm* 152-153)

He also has a sensitive side, caring for a nun and her orphanage and trying to avoid looking at the faces of those he's killed. At the same time, he craves action.

Jones tells him:

> C'mon, Storm, isn't it time for you to face reality? To face the fact that you aren't someone who can live off the grid. You need the action, the excitement, the adrenaline rush. Besides, in your heart, you're someone who cares – not only about helping people but about your country. You can put on that tough guy mask for the likes of Agent April Showers, but you don't fool me. Clara Strike saw through it, too. That's why I had her recruit you to work for us. It's why I need you now. (*A Bloody Storm,* ch. 4)

Of course, Storm is also a flirt – the James Bond type who always gets the girl. Besides Clara Strike, the bad girl/Elektra figure in his life, he generally has a different "good girl" partner each book. He's always quite charming and flirtatious with her. "He sounded sincere. He was very good at sounding sincere. It had always served him well – at work and in bed" (*A Brewing Storm,* ch. 4). In *Wild Storm,* he gallantly refuses to sleep with the archeological student he's saved, Katie Comely. Other times, however, he takes all that's offered, or at least he tries.

He's good looking but rather beat up:

> Storm was still ruggedly handsome, although his body also was showing the signs of his past. Five scars in his abdomen marked where he'd been shot. There was a knife wound on his back where he'd been slashed from behind. More recently, a bullet had ice-skated across

> his shoulder, leaving an ugly superficial scar. Of course, the worst wounds had been delivered in Tangiers – physically and mentally. (*A Raging Storm*, ch. 4)

This is where he nearly died, and the world believed he did.

A Calm Before Storm begins with Derrick Storm selling out his practice to bigshot Jake Palace and buying a luxury yacht. He ends it crashing the cruiser and reenlisting in the CIA as he'll need the money. In *Unholy Storm*, he's nearly penniless once more and taking unsavory jobs. One assumes he'll continue forever, in a holding pattern with Clara, finances, work and morality, always ready for another adventure.

Clara Strike

Storm meets his ex-girlfriend on many missions, as they're both contractors for the CIA. Each of them has "died," (or at least, the CIA faked their deaths). When Clara dies in Storm's arms he's devastated, and afterwards, when she returns from death in *Storm Season*, he can't fully trust her.

> It was an ironic twist. Clara had been declared dead once, too. There was even a death certificate filed in Richmond that verified she had been killed. He'd believed it when Jones had first told him. He'd been crushed. She'd been ripped from his life, and for one of the first times in his memory, he'd grieved. He'd actually felt tremendous and overwhelming loss because of her death.
>
> Then he'd discovered it was a lie. Jones had engineered it. Her death was for the good of the company. For the good of the country. But it had not been for his good. It had taken him a long time to accept that Clara had not died, that she had been somewhere breathing, eating, possibly making love with someone else, while he was grieving. Yet she had not contacted him. She'd let him believe that she had been killed. Why? Being dead seemed to be an occupational hazard

> when you worked for Jones. It was a professional
> requirement; only her death had cut him deep.
> Storm wondered, Had his death caused the same
> reaction in her? (*A Brewing Storm*, ch. 2)

Further, upon her return she abandons him to die, airily claiming that she knew he could handle it. They hook up on cases, but the relationship is volatile – often they find themselves on opposite sides, as Clara Strike tries to retrieve a deadly weapon and Storm is determined to destroy it in *Wild Storm*.

They still have a great deal of chemistry and she's the one great love of his life. He finds her perfume truly intoxicating. Storm thinks: "He and Clara Strike had a complicated history like two quarreling clans whose members kept intermarrying. Sometimes they made love. Sometimes, they made war. The only constant was the passion behind both impulses" (*Wild Storm* 169-170). They are unable to ever settle down or break out of their patterns, always putting the mission before each other.

Carl Storm

Derrick's father is a retired FBI agent who still keeps tabs on his son. He still has many contacts he can use at need, and plenty of field experience. Carl spends his time building models of old CIA buildings – useful to Storm when he finds himself inside one in *Deadly Storm*. Derrick Storm notes that his father's morality is a major factor in how he makes choices. Carl ends *Wild Storm* attending an Orioles game with his son, as Major League Baseball was always a bonding moment between them.

When Carl picks a fight with Clara, Derrick walks out and Carl notes, "He doesn't always do well watching people fighting. Especially when it's people he cares about" (*A Calm Before Storm*). In *Storm Front*, he watches Derrick's back from out on his farm where he works on cars for entertainment. He always refuses to tell Derrick anything about his mother, until in *A Calm Before Storm* they find themselves teamed up and hunting down her killer.

Jedidiah Jones

"Although Jones was old enough to be Storm's father, the NCS director was military-fit, built like a pit bull, with a shaved head and a raspy voice that sounded angry even when he was paying a compliment, which was rare" (*A Brewing Storm*, ch. 2).

Jones is heartless and opportunistic, always using Storm and Strike for his own agenda and never sharing the full picture. He's always eager to acquire weapons technology, though Derick Storm believes some secrets should remain buried forever.

April Showers

Storm's partner for all three novellas is the red-haired, green-eyed FBI Agent April Showers. She's incredibly capable, even while injured. As Storm notes while profiling her:

> "Editor of the *Georgetown Law Review,* top in your graduating class at the FBI Academy in Quantico. The Bureau sent you to Seattle first, but you were too good to stay long in the field. The brass wanted you at headquarters. The best and brightest. A go-to agent in high-profile cases. Smart. Clever. Someone who understood this city. A workaholic. No time for hobbies. No time for fun. No time for marriage or even a boyfriend. Your mother doesn't like that. She wants grandkids."
>
> "There's nothing in my personnel record about my mother wanting grandkids," she said.
>
> "Doesn't need to be. Flaming red hair. Emerald eyes. You've got Irish written all over your face. I've never met an Irish mother, especially a good Catholic, who didn't want her only daughter married and pregnant. She must be so disappointed." (*A Brewing Storm*, ch. 7)

She in turn points out that she likes the rules, unlike

cowboys like Storm:

> "When I was in college, a CIA recruiter came to see me. He told me that people who worked for the Agency were not obligated to follow U.S. laws when they traveled overseas. He bragged that a CIA employee could lie, cheat, steal, break into apartments, and even kill. The rules don't apply. That's what he said. That's the sort of folks he wanted working for him. People who think they are above the law. People like you." (*A Raging Storm*, ch. 7)

Real World Books

Derrick Storm Novels and Novellas (really in print)
- *A Brewing Storm*   (2012)
- *A Raging Storm*   (2012)
- *A Bloody Storm*   (2012)
- *Storm Front*   (2013)
- *Wild Storm*   (2014)

Derrick Storm Graphic Novels (really in print, allegedly adapted from Castle's old books)
- *Deadly Storm*   (2011)
- *Storm Season*   (2012)
- *A Calm Before Storm*   (2013)
- *Unholy Storm*   (2014)

One of his assignments had gone terribly wrong. Tangiers! It had ended with Storm lying severely wounded on a cold floor in his own blood.

Jones had rescued him. Storm had survived, but Tangiers had changed him. After that, he'd decided that he wanted out. And the only way for him to quit was for Derrick Storm – the roguish private eye and conscripted CIA operative – to die. In poetic fashion, he'd gone out in much the same way that he'd come into Jones's world. Storm had perished in the arms of Clara Strike. She'd watched in stunned disbelief as the light in his eyes dimmed. He'd reached out for her, and she had

> taken his hand, squeezing it for the very last time. His
> death had seemed legitimate because it had been as
> close to a real death as possible – thanks to the wizards
> inside the CIA's Chief Directorate of Science and
> Technology. The CIA scientists had used their magic to
> stop his heart and show no discernible brain waves.
> Storm didn't know how they'd done this. He hadn't
> cared. Death had freed him. (*A Raging Storm*, ch. 4)

Derrick Storm returns from death in a trilogy of
novellas that reveal his death was faked by the CIA and
he's been in hiding in Montana. "Four years of solitude.
Of peace. Of self-assessment. Of reevaluation and
reflection" ("A Brewing Storm," ch.1). Now all that has
ended, as his handler, Jedidiah Jones, summons him out of
retirement.

> The speaker hollered, "Jedidiah says he's calling in
> Tangiers." Tangiers. Tangiers had been bad. Even after
> all of these years, whenever the fisherman thought of
> Tangiers, he could still feel the cold linoleum pressed
> against his cheek, sticky and wet with his own blood. He
> could still see the mangled bodies and hear the
> unanswered cries for help. If it weren't for Jedidiah . . .
> Reeling in his line, the man started toward the creek
> bank. He did not talk to the two strangers waiting there.
> He gathered up his gear and boarded the helicopter.
> Tangiers. It was a hell of an IOU to call in. Jedidiah
> knew how difficult it had been for him to disappear. To
> go off-the-grid. To die, at least to be dead to a world that
> he had once known. A world that had tried to kill him,
> not once, but many, many times. Jedidiah understood
> why it had been important for him to no longer exist.
> And now Jedidiah was calling him back, dragging him
> back, to what he had worked so hard to free himself
> from. ("A Brewing Storm," ch.1)

Derrick Storm unwillingly comes out of apparent
death to investigate a political crime in Washington DC.

> "Who's been kidnapped?" Storm asked.

97

> "The stepson of a U.S. senator," Jones replied. "His name is Matthew Dull, and his stepfather is Senator Thurston Windslow from Texas."
>
> Thurston Windslow. The first player in the Kabuki play that was about to begin. Windslow was one of the most powerful senators on Capitol Hill and chair of the U.S. Select Committee on Intelligence – the oversight committee charged with keeping an eye on the CIA and Jedidiah Jones. No wonder Jones was interested. But there had to be other players and more to this than a kidnapping. (*A Brewing Storm*, ch. 2)

A Brewing Storm ends on a cliffhanger as one criminal is apprehended, but the larger force remains loose – a Russian oligarch about whom Jedidiah Jones knows more than he's telling. In the second book, Storm pursues him to London to discover his secrets and end up caught in a violent grab for power. *A Bloody Storm* sends him with a small team to Uzbekistan in search of a stockpile of gold – and a traitor among them. With car chases, torture, murder and more, the books are short but action-packed.

Following this, Storm returns more officially in *Storm Front* (2013), a real world novel dedicated to Richard Castle's father and presumably inspired by his spy time in "Hunt" (516). In it, Agent Kevin Bryan and Agent Javier Rodriguez join the team, working for Storm's CIA handler Jedidiah Jones. Captain Roy Montgomery is a heroic plane captain. And Storm meets Heat and Jameson, in a delightful moment for everyone.

In *Storm Front*, Volkov, a brutal hitman who enjoys torture, is Storm's nemesis. A millionaire on the verge of ruin has tried to disrupt the world's economy, but Volkov, whom he hired, decides to take matters into his own hands. Rook saves the day and makes sure the millionaire donates enough to save an orphanage in Romania that's going under. Ling Xi Bang (sounding like She Bang) is the good girl. She's a Chinese agent trying to save the world from financial ruin as Storm is. When she goes undercover, he enjoys dressing her as a dirty schoolgirl and sending her in as a hapless intern cute enough to seduce a senator (*Storm Front* 159). His ex, Clara Strike, shows up as the bad girl. With the two girls (one believed dead), the nemesis returned from the dead, and the CIA operative (also returned from the dead) this has many *James Bond* tropes.

Wild Storm begins with a plane crash – three commercial airlines go down, but with his customary heroics, Derrick Storm saves the one he's on. Flights are grounded when it's discovered a pair of small, incredibly powerful lasers is targeting planes from the ground, one in the US and one in the Middle East. While Storm's handler Jedidiah Jones wants him to capture the technology for the US, Storm is determined to destroy it. He and Clara Strike are sent to Egypt to explore a dig that may have discovered the rarest of rare earths, Promethium. The pieces of the puzzle slowly fuse into a whole as a kidnapped scientist, a luxury yacht, and a gambling trip to Monaco all give the story a classic Bond flavor.

Comic Books

Since ABC, Hyperion and Marvel are owned by Disney, the *Castle* team began making Derrick Storm comics, available through Marvel. Comic veterans Peter David, Brian Michael Bendis and Kelly Sue DeConnick wrote some of them.

> Show creator Andrew Marlowe, says that doing a Derrick Storm graphic novel allowed them to dig into Castle's "earlier works" in a different way. But he doesn't want to do spinoffs for spinoffs' sake. "We're looking to actually expand the Castle world and bring experiences to the audience that they're really, really going to enjoy," Marlowe says. (Truitt)

Deadly Storm is meant to be the first of the Storm novels, "adapted" like several others into comic books and graphic novel collections. A suspicious wife hires Storm to track down Jefferson Grout and discover if he's cheating.

Storm finds the man and dodges shots, only to get a prompt visit from Clara Strike of the CIA. In fact, Grout (actually Daniel Sanchez) was their operative, now on the run and expert at evading capture. The CIA wants Storm to find him again, as they're forbidden to operate on US soil. Storm begins by investigating the "wife," only to be arrested for her murder. He tails Grout to Nicaragua, only to end up in a fight for his life as he stumbles into Clara Strike's operation. They team up, necessitating time spent undressed in a hotel room, undercover. Clara is shot and he refuses to leave her, so she dies in his arms…or so it appears. A year later, Storm has used the profits from Nicaragua to expand his business. Helen Pierce signs up as his CIA handler as they head off to close Clara's cases together. As Storm thinks, "From deadbeat gumshoe and perennial disappointment to owner and operator of NYC's most glamourous boutique detective agency in one year. And did I mention the part about being a secret CIA op? My life does not suck."

Storm Season has Derrick Storm on the job for the CIA, and after, a man comes to him seeking his sister, who's been imprisoned by the African warlord Mawatu. However, as he goes undercover, Storm bumps into Clara Strike, alive and well. She leaves him to die, but tells him after that she knew he could handle it. Meanwhile, the patriots of the Congo are trying to destroy Mawatu, and Storm finally wins two of them over by reminding them they are meant to be patriots not thugs. His assistant is captured by Mawatu's men and she leads an escape of the many women he has captured. They band together to take him down in court after.

In *A Calm Before Storm,* Derrick Storm discovers the decapitated head of a victim of the criminal The Fear. His father, Carl, reveals this was the criminal who killed his mother. After charging in, Carl and Derrick are framed for the murder, and their CIA contact Helen Pierce must bail them out. Derrick finds himself parachuting over Russia, only to realize that he's never done it before and is in fact terrified. He and his father follow Clara Strike in to kill The Fear, only to discover that he's planning an assassination on the hundred-year anniversary of the Bloody Sunday massacre – he will kill the Russian president and open fire on the people with German weapons to stage another war. But as Fear uses them against each other, their chance to stop him grows bleak.

Unholy Storm begins with the murder of four young women, all wealthy, all marked with crossed daggers. As in the novellas, Storm is hired to get to the bottom of the crime by any means necessary. He traces the crimes to New Orleans and invites Clara Strike along. There, they find themselves embroiled in voodoo, menaced by zombies controlled by a seductive priestess, Mama Seraphina. At last, Storm discovers the reason each victim is marked with the *loa* Lenglensou, punisher of those who reveal secrets. The *Tonton Macoute,* Haitian president's personal guard and punishers of the innocent, were involved, wielding the powers of dark magic against their enemies. Today they call themselves the Sword and Razor, toppling governments with their power and making illicit bargains…until they return to collect.

After all these adventures, Storm dies in *Storm Fall* (as shown in episode one of the show). To break the fourth wall even farther open, The *Derrick Storm* series is now set to be adapted into its own TV series by ABC, with Andrew W. Marlowe and Terri Edda Miller as showrunners once again.

Genre Episodes

Of course, most episodes enter the tiny subcultures hidden within New York: dog shows, pizzerias, talk show hosts, zombie cosplayers. But a few push further, celebrating the biggest fan genres

Mystery

Castle plays poker with real mystery writers: Stephen J. Cannell, James Patterson, Dennis Lehane, and Michael Connelly appear as themselves. On September 30, 2010, Cannell died in real life, and the characters kept his chair empty in homage. The real *Heat Rises* afterward reads: "There is an empty chair at my weekly poker game. Connelly, Lehane, and I decided to keep dealing you in, Mr. Cannell, and somehow you keep winning. As it was in life, my friend and mentor. You had me at Rockford" (304). Castle describes liking many mystery and spy authors as well as the classics:

> Props to the Hardy Boys, Nancy Drew and Tom Swift. Rex Stout, Conan Doyle, Agatha Christie, Ian Fleming, le Carré, Poe, J.K. Rowling, Connelly, Robert Parker, Homer, Frank Miller, Alan Moore, Neil Gaiman, Ellery Queen, Stephen King, Bob Dylan, Rimbaud, Wallace Stevens and H.A.& Margret Rey. (Richardcastle.net)

In a further homage, the 12th Precinct of the NYPD is the same precinct used in the 1970s police sitcom *Barney Miller*. More quick nods to other series are sprinkled through the text.

> **Castle:** We make a pretty good team, you know. Like Starsky and Hutch, Tango and Cash... Turner and Hooch.

Beckett: You know, now that you mention it, you do remind me a little of Hooch. ("Deep in Death," 201)

Castle: This feels different, doesn't it?
Beckett: What does?
Castle: Rolling up to a crime scene as a married couple. Like Nick and Nora Charles.
Beckett: Ooh, like MacMillan and wife.
Castle: Hart to Hart.
Beckett: Turner and Hooch.
Castle: Turner and Hooch aren't even married.
Beckett: Yeah, but you still remind me a little of Hooch. ("Kill Switch," 708)

A scene from *Heat Rises* has Jameson Rook go instantly to the novels he's read:

> One of the messages was from the travel agent I referred Captain Montrose to. She said she can't believe the news, especially since she just talked to him yesterday. He booked an island cruise."
>
> "Yesterday?" When she affirmed, he clapped his hands once and said, "John le Carre!" He read her bewilderment and added, "You know John le Carre, right? *Spy Who Came in from the Cold, Constant Gardener...* Oh, and *A Perfect Spy* – transcendent, best ever! But...John le Carre's first novel was *Call for the Dead.* This secret agent is found. Suicide, they say. But that theory unravels because he left a wake-up call the night before. See the logic? Who leaves a wake-up call if he plans to kill himself?"
>
> "Right," she said. "And who books a cruise? Especially Montrose." (*Heat Rises* 147)

According to Andrew Marlowe's commentary, after Castle says that this is the coolest case ever ("A Deadly Game," 224), Montgomery was supposed to say "You think this is cool? Do you have any idea the amount of paperwork this just created? See, this is why I can't watch action movies. Shootouts, car chases, explosions. I sit in the theater and all I can think about is the damn paperwork someone's gonna have to fill out."

> **Castle:** Sure. Wow, nice. You know I was thinking on the way over here. All the best cops, *Dirty Harry, Cobra*, guy from *Police Academy* who makes the helicopter noises. They all have one thing in common.
> **Beckett:** Plucky sidekick?
> **Castle:** That and they do their very best work after they've been booted off a case. ("Knockout," 324)

On their first meeting, Castle attaches himself to Beckett the brilliant detective, to learn her methods and write about her as he plays sidekick – this is very Holmes and Watson. She's the pragmatist, and he romanticizes everything, especially in his writing. Castle also reads her from her accessories and body language – Sherlock's big party trick. He does something similar to 3XK. References continue through the series, as Slaughter calls Castle "Sherlock" for the entire episode ("Headhunters" 421).

> **Castle:** I could get a bloodhound. I could name him Sherlock, and then I could – I could bring him to crime scenes.
> **Beckett:** No, you couldn't.
> **Castle:** Oh, what? It'd be adorable. I could get him to wear a little Sherlock hat, train him how to carry a little magnifying glass. Oh, see? Right there. Disapproving, judgmental. You're totally my work wife. ("The Fifth Bullet," 211)

> **Beckett:** Okay Castle, I'm here; what's so important?
> **Castle:** Your first clue is: "The Curious Incident of the Dog in the Nighttime".
> **Beckett:** Oh, Jeez, Castle, I haven't even had my coffee yet - (*he hands her a cup of coffee*) Thank you.
> **Castle:** From the Sherlock Holmes stories, *Silver Blaze*. Holmes unmasks the murderer because of what didn't happen. The dog didn't bark. That's how he knew: the dog must have known the killer. ("Murder Most Fowl," 308)

In season seven, Beckett gives her new PI husband a gift of deerstalker hat and magnifying glass ("Castle, P.I.,"

711) and Castle arranges to speak at the Sherlock Holmes Society ("In Plane Sight," 721).

In the sleepy coastal village of the Hamptons, Castle discovers a murder. The title and in-show references strike a clear homage during "Murder, He Wrote" (505).

> **Castle:** Anyway, I need your guys' help. There has been a homicide out here in the Hamptons in my backyard.
> **Ryan:** Seriously, Castle? What, are you in an episode of *Murder, She Wrote*?
> **Castle:** More like Murder, He Wrote. But unfortunately, unlike Jessica Fletcher, the local police chief? Not a friend of mine and I think he might have the wrong guy. So, I need you guys to question the victim's wife in the city. Find out what she knows.

Storm and Strike meet in the bar of the Winter Palace in Luxor, Egypt, where Agatha Christie was said to have written *Death on the Nile* (*Wild Storm* 171). In another echo, the season seven story arc of Castle's mysterious disappearance, and the convenient amnesia that followed may be an homage to Agatha Christie. The in-universe rumors that he faked his disappearance to walk away from a relationship or as a publicity stunt also echo Christie's experience.

Hard Boiled

In his introduction to *Storm Season*, Castle describes Derrick Storm influences including Raymond Chandler and Mickey Spillane. Describing internet research, Rook says he's "Not exactly Philip Marlowe gumshoeing bad guys in *The Big Sleep*, but it has its rewards. I can snack, for instance" (*Heat Rises* 201). Indeed, Castle shows heavy noir influence in some of his writing and discussions of it:

> **Castle**: Good enough to be our perp?
> **Ryan**: Why do you writers always call them perps?
> **Castle**: Isn't that what you call them?
> **Ryan**: Aah, we got a lot of names for 'em.

Esposito: Yeah.
Ryan: Pipehead, pisshead, ork, creep.
(Castle takes out a notepad and starts jotting down.)
Esposito: Crook, knucklehead, chucklehead.
Ryan: Chud, turd.
Esposito: Destro, skell.
Ryan: Skeksi, slicko, slick.
Esposito: Mope.
Ryan: Sleestak.
Castle: Slow down, slow down.
Beckett: Suspects. We call them suspects.
Roy: I'm old school. I like 'dirtbag'.
Castle: Classic. ("Home is Where the Heart Stops," 107)

"A Slice of Death" (320) is an homage to the noir genre with passwords like Sam Spade. Even the episode's twist is a shout-out to *The Usual Suspects*.

Private Eye Joe Flynn opens the episode "The Blue Butterfly" (414) with his own hardboiled narration. Playing him, Nathan Fillion and his friends do a story firmly planted in the forties. Period music, costumes, and lighting set the scene. It's soon revealed that Castle is reading a diary, investigating a murder of the past.

> **Castle**: Uh, this diary in Stan's stuff. It's also from the '40s. It sounds like it belonged to a private eye. Listen to this. "Usually the wives turn on the waterworks when shown pictures of their husbands stepping out, but not this dame. She wanted payback. So what's worse? That I pitched woo with a client, or that I billed her for services rendered after?"
> **Beckett:** Cute.
> **Castle:** Cute? I mean, this guy sounds like a hard boiled PI right out of a Raymond Chandler novel. I wonder why Stan had this.

A blue butterfly diamond necklace that's worth a million dollars and said to be cursed is at the center of the story, as Joe falls for Vera, girlfriend to a mob boss. On finding Joe and Vera were murdered, Castle notes, getting into the mood, "Damn it, Joe. You old sap. Dizzy with a dame and got yourself cooked." Ryan even calls Castle "Mr. Bogart."

In season seven, Castle starts his own PI agency and instantly hurls himself into the genre, narrating for his tape recorder: "We were all after the same thing: justice. Trouble is, when it came to me, Lady Justice had different plans. While Beckett and the boys closed in on the killer I'd been kicked to the gutter like yesterday's trash. It just didn't seem fair" ("Castle, P.I.," 711). In the next episode, he gets a case, still while narrating:

> **Castle**: It was 11 in the morning. My phone was quieter than a dead church mouse. My head hurt after hitting the sauce like there was no tomorrow. For all I knew, there was no tomorrow. I was about to pour a smile in my coffee, have a little hair of the dog that bit me when she walked in.
> **Sohia:** Señor Castle. I'm looking for a private investigator. ("Private Eye Caramba!" 712)

Castle begins doing legwork the old-fashioned way, though he gets some flirting in with his favorite detective.

> **Beckett:** Ready to get out of here? Call it a night?
> **Castle**: Whoa, what's the rush, doll? Why don't you stick around a while, give those stems of yours a rest?
> **Beckett** (playing along): Could I? I'm all alone, and this is my first time in the big, scary city.
> **Castle**: Spare me the tell-tale, precious. A dame like you, you got an angle.
> **Beckett:** You're pretty quick for a gumshoe.
> **Castle**: Come on, spill the story. Time is money, and I got none of either.
> **Beckett:** All right, I'll give it to you straight. I'm just a girl, looking for a private dick. (grabs him)
> **Castle**: Whoah! Then your search is over, sweetheart. ("Private Eye Caramba!" 712)

He also compares his search to the quest for the Maltese Falcon. As is typical for the genre, his bad-girl client has been lying and using him for her own agenda and points a slender pistol at him. Nonetheless, he solves the case and walks out into the night with his favorite gal.

> **Castle**: As the sun set on the mean streets of the naked city, I could feel my luck was about to change. The killer was caught, my case was closed, and hanging on my arm was the dame of my dreams.
> **Beckett:** Are you going to be doing that all night?
> **Castle**: Not if it hurts my chances. ("Private Eye Caramba!" 712)

Hitchcock Thriller

In a subtle nod to Hitchcock, the picture behind Castle's writing desk is a down-shot photo of a square spiral staircase, echoing *Vertigo*. There are several Hitchcockian episodes:

> **Castle:** Could it be that easy? "You take mine, I'll take yours."
> **Esposito:** What are you getting at, Castle?
> **Castle:** *Strangers on a Train.*
> **Ryan**: The Hitchcock movie?
> **Castle:** I'm partial to the novel by Patricia Highsmith, but yes. ("The Double Down," 202)

"The Lives of Others," (519) is a direct *Rear Window* story. Both heroes, with injured legs, are trapped in wheelchairs, observing a neighbor's murder through binoculars. "Hmm. You must be bored. You've actually gone *Rear Window*," Ryan notes. Beckett even wears a Grace-Kelly-style gown and perches in Castle's lap.

> **Castle:** I'm not crazy.
> **Beckett:** No. But you do have a vivid imagination. (she caresses his neck) And you've been stuck inside for two weeks. What were you doing looking out the window anyway?
> **Castle:** I was –
> **Beckett:** Bored? So you saw what you wanted to see? (he's silent) When did you take your last painkiller?
> **Castle:** I was not hallucinating.

> **Beckett:** C'mon, Castle. You're here with a broken leg, binoculars, seeing a Rear Window scenario playing across the way. I mean, what are the odds?
> **Castle:** (sad, low) Astronomical.
> **Beckett:** All right. I'm going to make us some dinner and then get you to bed.

In this episode, there are subtle references to other Hitchcock films: *Suspicion* (the female victim married a charming man and then fears her husband's intentions), *Rebecca* (the victim's name is DeWinter), *Rope* (with two conspirators executing a murder, then planting the evidence to throw police off their trail), and *Shadow of a Doubt* (crime in the family's home garage).

When Castle's PI client turns up dead and he witnesses the murder, he soon comes to doubt his impressions. He decides "This whole thing, it's a work of fiction. It's a – it's a Hitchcock movie with me cast as the witness. I'm Jimmy Stewart in *Vertigo*" ("I, Witness," 713). This is a film about a faked suicide which Jimmy Stewart's character is forced to witness. While the references are heavy-handed, Castle's certain he knows what's happening:

> **Castle:** There's no way Eva is really dead. In a classic Hitchcock-ian twist, it won't be her body. Mark my words.
> **Beckett:** Then who did we pull out of the river?
> **Castle:** Someone who could pass for Eva.
> **Beckett:** Okay, we'll run her prints. That should clear up whether it's Eva or not.
> **Castle:** Except her prints will be altered. Her face, unrecognizable. All part of Eva's plan to commit the perfect crime. You'll see.
> ...
> **Beckett:** (sighs) If Eva is a part of this setup then why is she in the morgue?
> **Castle:** Because, in classic Hitchcock fashion, her co-conspirator doubled crossed her.

The twists and turns are indeed Hitchcockian, as

multiple killers' schemes are revealed one by one.

Scifi

Firefly quips are common in the show and books. Rook and Storm, like Castle, are constantly identified as "Ruggedly handsome." Other quips on *Firefly* lines include a party in "Home is Where the Heart Stops" (107), at which the Mayor greets Castle with, "Why didn't you tell me you were gonna be at this shindig?" Castle says "Yeah, you better run" ("The Mistress Always Spanks Twice," 216) and "I was aiming for his head" ("Boom" 218) in similar circumstances to those on the show. He knows Chinese from a "TV show I used to love" ("Close Encounters of the Murderous Kind," 309) and Beckett wants something to make her feel "shiny," a *Firefly* line ("Lucky Stiff," 314). You haven't heard of the Serenity?" Castle's mom asks innocently about a spa ("Setup," 316). He looks up, quite startled. Famously, Gina Torres and Adam Baldwin guest-star.

Fillion adds, "The first time *Castle* put on gloves at a crime scene, they were blue: like "two two, hands of blue" I didn't ask, I just did it, and people live for that stuff. In the Halloween episode, I hid a prop from *Firefly* on the set [the catalyzer]. I put it on Twitter: can you spot it?" (Nussbaum). Nathan Fillion wears his *Firefly* outfit as his "space cowboy" Halloween costume ("Vampire Weekend," 206). Alexis notes that he wore it five years ago (for *Serenity)* and adds, "Don't you think you should move on?" Castle's co-worker compliments his shindig.

"The Final Frontier" (506) has Castle investigating a murder at SuperNova Con. "Shiny!" Castle exclaims. *Nebula 9's* "Captain Max Reynard," Lieutenant Chloe (Zoe), visits to the planet Ariel, and vicious cannibalistic "kreavers" (reavers) are *Firefly* nods. Castle thinks *Nebula 9* is silly, as it only lasted twelve episodes, ten years previously, though there's talk of a film. He mentions he's a Joss Whedon fan instead.

The novel authors take glee in slipping in similar references. For instance, Rook visits a strip club and the owner eyes him:

> "Sure, guess I could give you a bullwhip and a fedora. We'd market you as Indiana Bones. Or maybe go sci-fi. You sorta look like that guy who roamed outer space everybody's so crazy about."
> "Malcolm Reynolds?" asked Rook.
> "Who?...No, I'm thinking we give you a space helmet and some assless chaps and call you...Butt Rogers. (*Heat Rises* 244)

In the later Nikki Heat novels, detectives Malcolm and Reynolds assist. Rook says, "I can't put my finger on it, but there's something I like about Malcolm and Reynolds" (*Frozen Heat* 123). Doing a code search, "Rook even investigated a site devoted to the mutt languages of some TV series called *Firefly*" (*Deadly Heat* 88). While comparing himself to action figures, Rook says, "I know. *Firefly,* I sort of feel a connection to him. Can't explain it" (*Raging Heat* 15).

In his own mind, Fillion models himself after Harrison Ford and adds, "I steal all the best stuff from him" (Nussbaum). He peppers the show with *Star Wars* references, saying "Now I finally know what Obi wan Kenobi felt like when Darth Vader turned on him" ("The Dead Pool," 321) or complaining about Beckett and his mother pulling Jedi mind tricks on him ("The Late Shaft," 220), ("Secret's Safe with Me," 503). He and Alexis have a beloved set of lightsabers. At the local convention, she would play Leia, while he was Darth Vader ("The Final Frontier," 507). Castle wants a limited edition *Star Wars* lightsaber signed by George Lucas for Valentine's Day ("Reality Star Struck," 514).

Even his characters Rook and Storm reference the film. Rook says he slept with a reporter "once upon a time in a galaxy far far away" (*Frozen Heat* 81). When Nikki admits she's getting swept away in Rook's outlandish theories, he does a Darth Vader impression and calls her to "come to the Dark Side" (*Heat Rises* 265). Ordered to identify himself to US fighter jets, Storm explains that he's "just the orphaned nephew of a poor moisture farmer from the planet Tatooine" (*Wild Storm* 105).

"Punked," (304) is a "love letter to the Steampunk community." An LA Steampunk fan group even played extras in the episode. Castle explains steampunk to Beckett, describing it as "a subculture that embraces the simplicity and romance of the past and at the same time couples it with the hope and promise and sheer supercoolness of futuristic design."

The team find a murder victim shot with an antique bullet, as well as century-old clothing. While Castle believes instantly in time travel, they track his movements to a hidden steampunk club. The doorman stops them with Jules Verne trivia, which Castle guesses, of course. They find themselves in Victorian London, 1892, but with rock music, flashing lights, a penny-farthing with exhaust pipes, and a time machine. Their club president calls their club "an oasis where human potential and ingenuity is limitless. Where there's poetry and wonder and meaning even in death." Castle looks thrilled. The crime's solution is more prosaic, but they enjoy their time in the gilded world.

"Close Encounters of the Murderous Kind," (309) is the *X-Files* episode. Castle is clearly a fan, as he whistles the theme song whenever mysteries appear. Rob Bowman, who directed thirty-three episodes of *The X-Files* and the movie is a featured director and executive producer, while David Amann is a recurring writer. The story opens with spooky music and an astrophysicist dead from explosive decompression – as if she went to outer space.

> **Castle:** Check this out. She was reading *Taken By The Fourth Kind*. A book on alien abductions.
> **Beckett:** So what's your theory, Castle? That she was abducted and then killed by aliens?

Castle: Well... a story that makes more sense is...alien abduction gone wrong. One that ends with Marie accidently being blasted out of the airlock of the alien spaceship.

Of course, Beckett's comment about the real truth being out there is a reference to the show's tagline, "the truth is out there." Castle's comments about the aliens being grey, not green, shape-shifting aliens who only look human, Beckett dying her hair red and calling him "Mulder," and calling the Chinese spy the "cigarette smoking man" are all further nods to *X-Files*. Castle and Beckett are finally snatched from their car with bright lights overhead, but Castle discovers the culprits aren't aliens, but men in black.

Many production staff members at *Castle* got their start with *Star Trek*. The show also teams with visiting actors: Penny Johnson Jerald (Kasidy Yates) plays Chief Gates, Michael Dorn (Worf) is Beckett's psychiatrist, Tim Russ (Tuvok) plays Dr. Malcolm Wickfield, Nana Visitor (Major Kira) is Dr. Patty Barker. David Burke (Steven Price) appears as Chief John Brady, Robert Picardo (The Doctor) appeared as Doctor Death, and Ethan Phillips (Neelix) was in "The Final Nail" (315). Jonathan Frakes (William T. Riker) directed the episodes "Kill the Messenger" (208) and "The Final Frontier" (506), and "The Fast and the Furriest" (520), after directing Stana Katic in *The Librarian: The Curse of the Judas Chalice* (2008).

Checking his bucket list, Castle asks, "Can either one of you introduce me to Bill Shatner?" ("Scared to Death," 517). His outlandish theories include, "We are demonstrating two dimensional thinking here, like Khan in *Star Trek 2: Wrath of Khan*" ("Deep Cover," 612). "The Final Frontier," (506) is a clear homage with its title, while its fictional show, Nebula 9, appears a mash-up between *Star Trek* and old-school *Battlestar Galactica*. Castle imitates Kirk and Picard and chortles that the victim was killed by a phaser. Jonathan Frakes cameos as a fan and Armin

Shimerman (Quark of *Star Trek: DS9*) designs fannish weapons as yet another unscrupulous dealer. On the mission to Mars episode, Castle likewise goes straight to fandom, narrating: "Space - the final frontier. These are the voyages of Castle and Beckett. Their ongoing mission: to explore strange, new motives; to seek out new witnesses, new suspects for murder; to boldly go... Oh, right over here" ("The Wrong Stuff," 716).

Of course on the Mars mission, he's delighted to wear a spacesuit. The story turns into a *2001: A Space Odyssey* death trap, and Castle is quick to out-logic the computer. It even features Castle saying "Open the pod bay doors." He adds, "There goes my *Rise of the Machines* theory" and "Is it just me, or does this remind you of *Alien*?"

> **Castle:** No, it didn't just walk out on its own. Beckett, you were right. The killer isn't the devil. The devil doesn't need to dispose of evidence.
> **Beckett:** Clearly.
> **Castle:** Clearly is the perfect word because clearly our killer is the invisible man. ("Clear & Present Danger," 703)

Castle theorizes the Invisible Man when security cameras don't pick up the killer ("Clear & Present Danger," 703). However, his theory comes true when they're attacked at a crime scene by someone invisible.

> **Castle:** Quantum engineering? DARPA? You are researching invisibility.
> **Sarkov:** No, Mr. Castle. Invisibility is science fiction.
> Castle scoffs. He's not convinced.
> **Sarkov:** Cloaking, however, is science.

The invisibility is actually caused by a suit, which uses quantum cellular equations derived from cephalopods. There are other scifi nods (as usual) as Castle defends them with training from Zombie Apocalypse camp as well as infrared goggles and Beckett must tell him, "You just kind of make nerdy…sexy." The co-inventor of the suit is also a geek, telling Castle, "We both realized that I had become Frodo. And the suit was the one ring to rule them all. Will knew it was too much power for anyone to have, especially the government….It needed to be destroyed. Cast into the fires of Mordor."

The time travel episode ("Time Will Tell," 605) uses all the clichés: A suspect, Simon Doyle, insists he's from the future, traveling back to stop a murder that will alter the timeline.

> **Simon:** Look. After the bloody energy wars of 2031 we finally managed to cultivate new sources of power.
> **Castle:** Energy wars?
> **Simon:** Yeah, neofacists come to power and try to control the world's energy supply for a select few. Don't worry. We defeat them. Turns out, one of these new sources of power is a tachyon generator. It lets us open doors in the time stream continuum allowing us to travel back in time. But of course, because of the possibility of abuse it was tightly regulated and kept secret from the public.

Since he insists he's a temporal anthropologist who travels back in time to study culturally significant eras, Castle asks about the butterfly effect. Esposito shows his own geek cred by calling the suspect's strange gadget "Doctor Who's sonic screwdriver." He also sarcastically points out the suspect's story is derivative of *Twelve Monkeys* and *The Terminator*. The former follows a time traveler from the post-apocalyptic future who goes back in time to eradicate the source of a deadly plague The latter sees a future criminal travel back in time to wipe out humanity's future savior's mother.

In a *Terminator*-like plot, the criminal here has traveled back to find a twenty-one-year-old psychics student named Paul Deschile. Doyle realizes he is the target he's come to save:

116

> The energy wars, all right? I told you about the other side. A group of fascists. They were worse than the Nazis. They were slaughtering people by the tens of thousands, okay? They were winning. Until Deschile. He and his team, they – they created an energy shield, okay? It was able to stop their weapons. It completely turned the tide. (he slams his hands on her desk) Detective, listen to me! Ward is still out there, obviously fighting for the fascists. They trying to win the war by rewriting history! And if he kills Deschile there will be no energy shield. And without that energy shield we lose that war! Ward's going to kill Deschile and that is why billions of people die!

The episode ends with Beckett spilling coffee on the letter the criminal from the future used to track Paul Deschile, then discovering it perfectly matches the stained copy he had. The time loop is closed. When Simon disappears from lockup, Beckett asks where he is and Castle responds with "Not where, when," a nod to Inspector Spacetime's catchphrase. In fact, Fillion guest-starred on *Community*.

Horror

"Vampire Weekend," (206) begins on Halloween as a teenager is found with a stake in his heart in the cemetery. What follows is an exploration of vampire parties with their gothic drapings and candelabras (after the obligatory exploration of true vampires). But the truth is nearly as creepy. As a toddler, the victim witnessed his mother's gruesome murder, and has been drawing disturbing pictures of it with a dark, gothic tree. Under it is found evidence of his mother's real-life murder, revealing that his surfacing memories have led to the original murderer killing him and his best friend as well.

Nathan Fillion salutes his past works, as he wears his *Firefly* costume for Halloween. Nodding to his time as a *Buffy* villain, he patrols a graveyard and quips, "Looks like Buffy visited the Big Apple."

"Wrapped Up in Death" (219) takes Castle through the mummy's curse, as he gazes on the mummy of Kan-Xul, the legendary Mayan king in its sarcophagus and has ill-luck befall him (though some of it is his friends' pranks).

> **Bentley:** Tell them, Stanford. Tell them what was written at the entrance to the burial chamber. "All who gaze on the face of the Mayan king shall be struck down by his wrath."
> **Castle:** Mayan king? This Mayan king?
> **Bentley:** That very one. They all looked inside, and they're all dead.
> **Beckett:** There were other incidents?
> **Dr. Raynes:** All easily explainable. One of our grad students, Nicole Graham, was mauled to death by a jaguar outside the dig site.
> **Rachel:** And Professor Fisher died of dengue fever.
> **Dr. Raynes:** Which is common in that region, as are curses written above grave sites. It's how they kept people from robbing them for thousands of years.

Gil Birmingham, Cacaw Te, played a mummy's bodyguard in *Buffy's* "Inca Mummy Girl." Erick Avari from *The Mummy* (1999) also cameos. There is even evidence that the mummy is the murderer...or at least someone who handled mummies. "The mummy himself has risen from the grave and is roaming New York seeking vengeance," Castle decides. At episode end, Castle rids himself of the curse through ritual, only to suffer a "clumsy" cut in the kitchen.

"Mercy...I can see it. Mercy," cries Jack Sinclair, legendary ghost hunter, before he dies in the house he's investigating ("Demons," 406). He was locked in from the inside, and his throat was slit with the blood spraying everywhere...as if the killer was insubstantial. Rumors surround the mansion with "Lights going off, strange noises, doors slamming." There have been eight killings there, "starting with the original owner, Robert Pettigrew, strangled, 1903, all the way to Melanie Benton, hacked to pieces, 1991."

Beckett and Castle are locked in themselves, as the lights go out and strange noises appear, just as they did when Sinclair died. At last, they find a magnetic field generator that may be responsible...along with an unreported skeleton. This gives them a motive for the real murderer and the case is solved.

> **Beckett:** C'mon Castle. Even you have to admit everything, every haunting, every death, everything even remotely connected to paranormal activity in the McClaren house can be explained by that passageway.
> **Castle:** I don't know. What about last night, when we were in the living room? How about the door? The light? The candle?
> **Beckett:** Old wiring, drafty house.
> **Castle:** Well maybe it was something more. Think about it. If you hadn't gone looking for the draft that blew out the candle you would have never found the passageway or Matt Benton's body.
> **Beckett:** Spell it out for those of us that are...paranormally impaired.
> **Castle:** Maybe someone wanted us to find that passageway. Maybe Jack Sinclair's ghost was helping solve his own murder.

Esposito notes, "Only in New York could some guy dress like a friggin' zombie and walk down the street unnoticed" ("Undead Again," 422). Their victim was bitten and ripped off a cuff of an ancient shirt. Soon the team meet a man who's certain he's doomed to turn into a zombie and demands to be locked up. Another victim comes to life on their autopsy slab. "Is there a police code for zombie on the loose?" Castle asks as the man stumbles out.

At last, Beckett and Castle are mobbed on the street by the undead:

> **Castle:** That's – that's a – that's a zombie horde.
> **Beckett:** (unbelieving) There's no such thing as zombies.

> **Castle:** I'm sure I don't have to tell you to aim for the head....Beckett! Behind us. We're surrounded. Oh jeez, oh jeez. You don't have enough bullets. It's ground zero for *World War Z.*
> The zombies are getting closer.
> **Castle:** Get behind me. We'll have to fight our way out. Uh ...
> **Beckett:** There's no way this is real. NYPD! Stop moving, now!
> They're closing in on Castle, close enough to touch him.
> **Beckett:** And stop pretending to be zombies!
> The zombie horde slows slightly. The zombie that was leading the assault straightens.
> **Paul:** Hey, hey, hey, hey. Take it easy. We're just zombie walking here.

Castle instantly turns fan. In fact, among their subculture, some have been taking a zombielike hypnosis drug. One gives it to another to entice him to commit murder. In the end, Castle gets a confession by dressing as a zombie and terrorizing the real murderer.

"Scared to Death" (517) brings many contemporary horror movies into the fore, most notably *The Ring.* After he views a creepy video that vows he will die in three days, Castle even calls Wes Craven for advice on how to get out of his predicament.

> **Castle:** The name Wes Craven is synonymous with horror. You've made a fortune
> scaring the crap out of people. *My Soul to Take,* all the *Nightmare on Elm Streets* – terrifying.
> **Wes Craven:** So you call me up in the middle of the night to join my fan club? What?
> **Castle:** (sarcastically) Ha ha. No. I know that you've researched evil spirits who reach out from the beyond for all your films.
> **Wes Craven:** Well, of course.
> **Castle:** I was just wondering if you knew how to stop those pesky suckers.
> **Wes Craven:** Is this you making your own movie? I mean, are you writing a horror screenplay?
> **Castle:** Yes. I just thought I'd give you a little friendly competition. Just got a little writer's block is all.

Wes Craven: Okay, what's the story?
Castle: Um…ruggedly handsome hero and his notoriously practical lady friend watch a disc that's killing its viewers within three days.
Wes Craven: Really? You don't think that's a little derivative?
Castle: Yes…but…I am hoping to distinguish the ending. You know, make the third act a survival tale rather than a blood bath. I just can't figure out how to get my heroes out of this mess.
Wes Craven: So the key is always in the spirit's origin story. Once you have that you can start to figure out the spirit's weaknesses. If it's using the disc as its portal into our world, then–
Castle: Then the disc would contain clues as to the spirit's story. Wes, thank you! Thank you. Listen buddy, it's late. I gotta go.
Castle hangs up.
Wes Craven: Friendly competition my ass.

Castle knows his genre films and tells his friends:

Castle: The actual DVD will not kill me, Esposito. It will be the spirit inside the DVD. Just like in *The Ring.*
Ryan: Ooh, ooh, the one with the creepy, waterlogged little girl that crawls out of the TV. I didn't sleep for days after that movie.
Beckett: Yes! Exactly! Thank you. That movie. It's fiction. It's a horror story in a book about urban legends.
Ryan: Yeah. I mean, because that's…all it is, right? A legend.
Castle: Many legends are based in truth. I saw the video. At midnight in three days' time I will die.

He refuses to sleep with Beckett because "In every horror movie I've ever seen, having sex pretty much guarantees we will die. So for the safety of us both, I say we just…hold off." In addition, Castle and Beckett visit a suspect in a mental hospital in a scene reminiscent of *Silence of the Lambs*, in which they're told to stay away from the glass. Eventually, they trek up to the forest seeking the next victim. Once again, Castle reveals his familiarity with the genre:

Castle: Uh…we're going to a cabin in the woods in the middle of nowhere.
Beckett: Yeah, so?
Castle: So it's like the coed checking out the strange noise in the basement in a slasher flick. It's a recipe for disaster.

He's certain he won't survive, as he's the comic relief guy. In a showdown in the utterly creepy woods, they discover the real murderer and survive the case.

Castle says, "Stephen King wrote stories of blood-thirsty cars and sold millions of copies. I figure, why be limited by logic?" ("The Fifth Bullet," 211). When he's certain a teen has the powers from *Carrie*, he's eager to call "Stephen" and tell him. In a school cafeteria, a table menaces a mean girl. Castle says, "The outcast. The mean girls. The rage that erupts in a telekinetic attack. This is a real life *Carrie*" ("Smells like Teen Spirit," 615). The head of the mean girls is killed, flung up to her ceiling. Jordan is traumatized by her own actions: "I got so angry and stuff just started flying around the cafeteria. And then I wished for Madison to be dead and the next thing I knew she was. It had to be me, right?" However, special effects are responsible, despite Castle's gullible nature.

Soap Opera

Angela: Joseph, this is the last time we can do this.
Joseph: What are you talking about?
Angela: I'm going back to my husband.
Joseph: Alfonso?
Angela: I'm sorry.
Joseph: Angie, baby, what about us?
[A door closes.]
Angela: Oh, my god. Oh, my god, that's him .He's home early.
Alfonso: Angela, are you upstairs?
Angela: Hide in the closet. Mi bello! ("One Life to Lose," 318)

As they continue acting their scene, Lance opens the closet to discover a real body there, complete with an axe in the back. Castle starts wildly speculating right away:

> **Castle**: Or maybe Sarah discovered that Greek billionaire Mikos had invented a machine that could cause blizzards that would plunge the entire world into an ice age.
> **Beckett**: Really? You're gonna go with an evil weather machine?
> **Castle**: It already happened. On *General Hospital.* Look, bear in mind, we're entering into a world of epic drama with larger than life characters, each one teaming with twisted secrets and personal intrigue. It stands to reason that the motive for this murder will be worthy of a soap opera.
> **Beckett**: Castle, even in a world of epic drama, the motives are usually quite ordinary.
> [They turn a corner and see the victim with the bright red fire axe in her back.]
> **Castle**: Now, does that look ordinary to you? The victim with an axe in her back on the set of her own show. Odds are, the killer walks amongst us on this very soundstage.

The actors' lives resemble a soap as everyone's sleeping with everyone else. Martha tells Castle, "Betrayal is a way of life on a soap opera. And, let me tell you, Temptation Lane is like this seething cauldron of sordidness, and treachery, and naked ambition. And do you know which people are the most manipulative and devious?" He decides he does – it's the writers. Of course, one of them is responsible.

The victim, another writer known for giving characters the axe, had her own soapy drama as her long lost mother reappeared in her life (actually a hoax). Castle protests that she's clearly "a gold digging opportunist who's insinuated herself back into her daughter's life because she's in need of a heart transplant and Sarah is the only compatible donor." Beckett retorts, "Sure, maybe on Temptation Lane. Not in the real world."

The soap episode nods to Nathan Fillion's past roles, as his first real role was Dr. Joey Buchanan on *One Life to Live* in 1995. The title salutes the show, as does visiting daytime soap star Cameron Mathison. Fillion adds, "I love running into actors who say 'Oh yeah, I did a soap.' I say 'Tell me which one!' It's like being a member of a secret society" (Nussbaum).

Along with Castle and his mother, Beckett is a fan and even defines shipping, celebrating the larger world of fandom even as she confesses her role as part of it.

Western

"Once Upon a Time in the West," (707) brings in every Western trope. The title is a Western film, of course, and Castle and Beckett ride a stagecoach to the Diamondback Old West Ranch in Arizona, "a living history resort where both staff and guest dress in old west attire and engage in cowboy activities." A *Bonanza*-style flaming map appears, as do Western opening credits. "It's like we rolled right into a John Ford movie," Castle smiles. They both change into cowboy outfits and Castle even buys matching six-shooters for them. In the bar he plays cards and even gets himself roughed up. He also reveals his love of the genre, as always:

> **Bartender:** What'll it be, fella?
> **Castle**: I'll take a cough and varnish.
> **Bartender:** Some what?
> **Castle**: You know, a gut warmer. Face burner. Nose paint? Cowboy cocktail? What do you all call whiskey here?
> **Bartender:** Whiskey.

Snooping around, the pair discovers their murder victim, Whitney, was tracing a legend of stolen gold for the past century. The bartender tells them, "Them Peacock Boys, they outrun a whole squad of soldiers by traversing Dead Man's Gorge. Two days later they was gunned down just outside of Phoenix. But the gold was gone." Whitney stole dynamite and went out riding to trace the lost gold, and Castle and Beckett do the same. When they find the real killer, he and Castle both finger their guns, preparing for a classic gunfight. However, Beckett arrives to shoot the gun from his hand in a tough black cowboy costume. She ends the episode by lassoing Castle in a white corseted dress, promising them a real honeymoon at last. The End appears in western lettering over their final kiss.

The Future

Fillion is entering unfamiliar territory. "This is the longest I've ever played a character without getting canceled," he says. "I'm curious where it's headed." (Sheffield)

New showrunners Alexi Hawley and Terence Paul Winter will be mixing things up in season eight – Beckett is captain now, and, without the chance to work cases beside her, Castle goes back to his PI business with a twist – Alexis insists on interning with him. "At the end of the day, we came into this season wanting to shake things up," new co-showrunner Alexi Hawley told *TVLine* at ABC's Television Critics Association press tour party. "The show has been doing a great job with what it's been doing, but now we've been given an opportunity to really sort of add some energy into it" (Mitovich, "Castle Bosses").

Captain Gates is gone, but new teammates include series regular security specialist Hayley Shipton (*The Neighbors'* Toks Olagundoye) and a recurring character of tech analyst Vikram Singh (*The Walking Dead*'s Sunkrish Bala). Stana Katic says of the new showrunners:

> "I started to feel the character would be safe in the next chapter of *Castle*. I felt confident that they knew the story, the character – Terence has been on the show since Day 1, and some of the most interesting episodes for my character were penned by Alexi – and while they are eager to shake things up and aim at telling challenging stories, they would also protect the integrity of the character." (Andreeva)

3XK is gone, along with his girlfriend and Senator Bracken, but there's far more to discover from the CIA and the secrets of Richard's disappearance. Castle is a PI again, with Alexis working cases on the street beside him. Beckett has taken over her old precinct. Back at the Attorney General's office, a dangerous mole is climbing to power, and Beckett will need to keep an eye on her old life, even as she tries to move forward with Castle. A dangerous time is coming, with secrets and surprises for all.

Episode List

Season 1

Episode #		Air Date	Title
1	101	09/Mar/2009	Flowers for Your Grave
2	102	16/Mar/2009	Nanny McDead
3	103	23/Mar/2009	Hedge Fund Homeboys
4	104	30/Mar/2009	Hell Hath No Fury
5	105	06/Apr/2009	A Chill Goes through her Veins
6	106	13/Apr/2009	Always Buy Retail
7	107	20/Apr/2009	Home is Where the Heart Stops
8	108	27/Apr/2009	Ghosts
9	109	04/May/2009	Little Girl Lost
10	110	11/May/2009	A Death in the Family

Season 2

Episode #		Air Date	Title
11	201	21/Sep/2009	Deep in Death
12	202	28/Sep/2009	The Double Down
13	203	05/Oct/2009	Inventing the Girl
14	204	12/Oct/2009	Fool Me Once...
15	205	19/Oct/2009	When the Bough Breaks
16	206	26/Oct/2009	Vampire Weekend
17	207	02/Nov/2009	Famous Last Words
18	208	09/Nov/2009	Kill the Messenger
19	209	16/Nov/2009	Love Me Dead
20	210	23/Nov/2009	One Man's Treasure
21	211	07/Dec/2009	The Fifth Bullet
22	212	11/Jan/2010	A Rose for Everafter
23	213	18/Jan/2010	Sucker Punch
24	214	25/Jan/2010	The Third Man
25	215	08/Feb/2010	Suicide Squeeze
26	216	08/Mar/2010	The Mistress Always Spanks Twice
27	217	22/Mar/2010	Tick, Tick, Tick... (1)

28	218	29/Mar/2010	Boom! (2)
29	219	05/Apr/2010	Wrapped Up in Death
30	220	12/Apr/2010	The Late Shaft
31	221	19/Apr/2010	Den of Thieves
32	222	03/May/2010	Food to Die For
33	223	10/May/2010	Overkill
34	224	17/May/2010	A Deadly Game

Season 3

Episode #		Air Date	Title
35	301	20/Sep/2010	A Deadly Affair
36	302	27/Sep/2010	He's Dead, She's Dead
37	303	04/Oct/2010	Under the Gun
38	304	11/Oct/2010	Punked
39	305	18/Oct/2010	Anatomy of a Murder
40	306	25/Oct/2010	3XK
41	307	01/Nov/2010	Almost Famous
42	308	08/Nov/2010	Murder Most Fowl
43	309	15/Nov/2010	Close Encounters of the Murderous Kind
44	310	06/Dec/2010	Last Call
45	311	03/Jan/2011	Nikki Heat
46	312	10/Jan/2011	Poof! You're Dead
47	313	24/Jan/2011	Knockdown
48	314	07/Feb/2011	Lucky Stiff
49	315	14/Feb/2011	The Final Nail
50	316	21/Feb/2011	Setup (1)
51	317	28/Feb/2011	Countdown (2)
52	318	21/Mar/2011	One Life to Lose
53	319	28/Mar/2011	Law & Murder
54	320	04/Apr/2011	Slice of Death
55	321	11/Apr/2011	The Dead Pool
56	322	02/May/2011	To Love and Die in L.A.
57	323	09/May/2011	Pretty Dead
58	324	16/May/2011	Knockout

Season 4

Episode #		Air Date	Title
59	401	19/Sep/2011	Rise
60	402	26/Sep/2011	Heroes & Villains

61	403	03/Oct/2011	Head Case
62	404	10/Oct/2011	Kick the Ballistics
63	405	17/Oct/2011	Eye of the Beholder
64	406	24/Oct/2011	Demons
65	407	31/Oct/2011	Cops & Robbers
66	408	07/Nov/2011	Heartbreak Hotel
67	409	21/Nov/2011	Kill Shot
68	410	05/Dec/2011	Cuffed
69	411	09/Jan/2012	Till Death Do Us Part
70	412	16/Jan/2012	Dial M for Mayor
71	413	23/Jan/2012	An Embarrassment of Bitches
72	414	06/Feb/2012	The Blue Butterfly
73	415	13/Feb/2012	Pandora (1)
74	416	20/Feb/2012	Linchpin (2)
75	417	27/Feb/2012	Once Upon a Crime
76	418	19/Mar/2012	A Dance With Death
77	419	26/Mar/2012	47 Seconds
78	420	02/Apr/2012	The Limey
79	421	16/Apr/2012	Headhunters
80	422	30/Apr/2012	Undead Again
81	423	07/May/2012	Always

Season 5

Episode #		Air Date	Title
82	501	24/Sep/2012	After the Storm
83	502	01/Oct/2012	Cloudy With a Chance of Murder
84	503	08/Oct/2012	Secret's Safe With Me
85	504	15/Oct/2012	Murder, He Wrote
86	505	29/Oct/2012	Probable Cause
87	506	05/Nov/2012	The Final Frontier
88	507	12/Nov/2012	Swan Song
89	508	19/Nov/2012	After Hours
90	509	03/Dec/2012	Secret Santa
91	510	07/Jan/2013	Significant Others
92	511	14/Jan/2013	Under the Influence
93	512	21/Jan/2013	Death Gone Crazy
94	513	04/Feb/2013	Recoil
95	514	11/Feb/2013	Reality Star Struck

96	515	18/Feb/2013	Target (1)
97	516	25/Feb/2013	Hunt (2)
98	517	18/Mar/2013	Scared to Death
99	518	25/Mar/2013	The Wild Rover
100	519	01/Apr/2013	The Lives of Others
101	520	15/Apr/2013	The Fast and the Furriest
102	521	22/Apr/2013	The Squab and the Quail
103	522	29/Apr/2013	Still
104	523	06/May/2013	The Human Factor
105	524	13/May/2013	Watershed

Season 6

Episode #	Air Date	Title
106 601	23/Sep/2013	Valkyrie (1)
107 602	30/Sep/2013	Dreamworld (2)
108 603	07/Oct/2013	Need to Know
109 604	14/Oct/2013	Number One Fan
110 605	21/Oct/2013	Time Will Tell
111 606	28/Oct/2013	Get a Clue
112 607	04/Nov/2013	Like Father, Like Daughter
113 608	11/Nov/2013	A Murder is Forever
114 609	18/Nov/2013	Disciple
115 610	25/Nov/2013	The Good, the Bad & the Baby
116 611	06/Jan/2014	Under Fire
117 612	13/Jan/2014	Deep Cover
118 613	20/Jan/2014	Limelight
119 614	03/Feb/2014	Dressed to Kill
120 615	17/Feb/2014	Smells Like Teen Spirit
121 616	24/Feb/2014	Room 147
122 617	03/Mar/2014	In the Belly of the Beast
123 618	17/Mar/2014	The Way of the Ninja
124 619	24/Mar/2014	The Greater Good
125 620	21/Apr/2014	That '70s Show
126 621	28/Apr/2014	Law & Boarder
127 622	05/May/2014	Veritas
128 623	12/May/2014	For Better or Worse

Season 7

Episode #	Air Date	Title

129	701	29/Sep/2014	Driven
130	702	06/Oct/2014	Montreal
131	703	13/Oct/2014	Clear and Present Danger
132	704	20/Oct/2014	Child's Play
133	705	27/Oct/2014	Meme is Murder
134	706	10/Nov/2014	The Time of Our Lives
135	707	17/Nov/2014	Once Upon a Time in the West
136	708	24/Nov/2014	Kill Switch
137	709	01/Dec/2014	Last Action Hero
138	710	08/Dec/2014	Bad Santa
139	711	12/Jan/2015	Castle, P.I.
140	712	19/Jan/2015	Private Eye Caramba!
141	713	02/Feb/2015	I, Witness
142	714	09/Feb/2015	Resurrection (1)
143	715	16/Feb/2015	Reckoning (2)
144	716	23/Feb/2015	The Wrong Stuff
145	717	16/Mar/2015	Hong Kong Hustle
146	718	23/Mar/2015	At Close Range
147	719	30/Mar/2015	Habeas Corpse
148	720	20/Apr/2015	Sleeper
149	721	27/Apr/2015	In Plane Sight
150	722	04/May/2015	Dead from New York
151	723	11/May/2015	Hollander's Woods

Works Cited

Primary Sources

Bendis, Brian Michael & Kelly Sue Deconnick. *Castle: Richard Castle's Deadly Storm,* New York: Marvel, 2013.
–. *Castle: Richard Castle's Storm Season.* New York: Marvel, 2012.
Bunn, Cullen, et. al. *Castle: Richard Castle's Unholy Storm.* New York: Marvel, 2014.
Castle: The Complete First Season. ABC Studios, 2009. DVD Boxset.
Castle: The Complete Second Season. ABC Studios, 2010. DVD Boxset.
Castle: The Complete Third Season. ABC Studios, 2011. DVD Boxset.
Castle: The Complete Fourth Season. ABC Studios, 2012. DVD Boxset.
Castle: The Complete Fifth Season. ABC Studios, 2013. DVD Boxset.
Castle: The Complete Sixth Season. ABC Studios, 2014. DVD Boxset.
Castle: Season Seven. ABC Studios, 2015. DVD Boxset.
Castle, Richard. *A Bloody Storm.* New York: Hyperion, 2012. Kindle.
–. *A Brewing Storm.* New York: Hyperion, 2012. Kindle.
–. *Deadly Heat.* New York: Hyperion, 2013.
–. *Driving Heat.* New York: Hyperion, 2015.
–. *Frozen Heat.* New York: Hyperion, 2012.
–. *Heat Rises.* New York: Hyperion, 2011.
–. *Heat Wave.* New York: Hyperion, 2009.
–. *Naked Heat.* New York: Hyperion, 2010.

—. *Raging Heat*. New York: Hyperion, 2014.

—. *A Raging Storm*. New York: Hyperion, 2012. Kindle.

—. *Storm Front*. New York: Hyperion, 2013.

—. *Wild Storm*. New York: Hyperion, 2014.

—. Richardcastle.net. http://www.richardcastle.net.

David, Peter and Robert Atkins. *Castle: Richard Castle's A Calm Before Storm*. New York: Marvel, 2014.

Secondary Sources

Andreeva, Nellie. "'Castle' Star Stana Katic On What Made Her Stay, Big Season 8 "Event" And Her Future On The Show & Beyond." *Deadline* 27 July 2015. http://deadline.com/2015/07/castle-stana-katic-season-8-abc-1201485528.

Bierly, Mandi, James Hibberd, and Jeff Jensen. "Nathan Fillion, Geek God." *Entertainment Weekly* 1147 (2011): 38-45. Academic Search Complete.

Highfill, Samantha. "Nathan Fillion Talks about 'Castle' Season 7 and his Dream Wedding" *Entertainment Weekly*. 26 Sept 2014 http://www.ew.com/article/2014/09/26/nathan-fillion-castle-season-7-preview

Mitovich, Matt Webb. *"Castle* Bosses Reveal Beckett's Big Move: 'We Wanted to Shake Things Up'" August 4 2015 http://tvline.com/2015/08/04/castle-season-8-beckett-captain.

—. *"Castle* Shocker: Penny Johnson Jerald Not Returning for Season 8." *TV Line* 29 May 2015 http://tvline.com/2015/05/29/castle-penny-johnson-jerald-leaving-gates-season-8.

Ng, Philiana. *"Castle* Creator: '100 Episodes Is a Miracle'." *The Hollywood Reporter* 31 March 2013. https://www.yahoo.com/tv/s/castle-creator-100-episodes-miracle-050000733.html?nf=1

—. *"Castle's* Jack Coleman: Bracken's Return Puts Beckett in a Moral Quandary." *The Hollywood Reporter* 4 Feb 2013. http://www.hollywoodreporter.com/live-feed/castle-jack-coleman-bracken-becketts-417802

Nussbaum, Emily. "The Vulture Transcript: Nathan Fillion on *Castle*, *Firefly*, and a *Dr. Horrible* Sequel" *Vulture.com*. 4 Oct 2010. http://www.vulture.com/2010/10/the_vulture_transcript_nathan.html

Sheffield, Rob. "*Castle* Is The New 'Rockford Files'." *Rolling Stone* 1166 (2012): 54. Academic Search Complete.

Truitt, Brian. "*Castle* Enters the Realm of Graphic Novels." *USA Today*: Academic Search Complete.

THE ESSENTIAL CASTLE

Index

About the Author

Valerie Estelle Frankel is the author of many books on pop culture, including *Doctor Who – The What, Where, and How, Sherlock: Every Canon Reference You May Have Missed in BBC's Series 1-3, History, Homages and the Highlands: An Outlander Guide,* and *How Game of Thrones Will End.* Many of her books focus on women's roles in fiction, from her heroine's journey guides *From Girl to Goddess* and *Buffy and the Heroine's Journey* to books like *Women in Game of Thrones* and *The Many Faces of Katniss Everdeen.* Once a lecturer at San Jose State University, she's a frequent speaker at conferences. Come explore her research at www.vefrankel.com.

Made in the USA
Lexington, KY
26 February 2017